Praise for

What Do I Do
with My Baby
All Day?!

"This is the best parenting book I've read in years. With its blend of developmental science, mindfulness, music, and movement, it's hugely original, creative, accessible, and full of humanity. It will be my go-to book for new parents from now on!"
—Arietta Slade, PhD, cofounder and codirector, Minding the Baby®, Child Study Center, Yale School of Medicine

"Vered Benhorin's gentle, authentic, and relatable style provides permission to embrace the complexity of becoming a mother. In a society that romanticizes motherhood, this book normalizes the struggle and the beauty of caring for a baby all in one. . . . *What Do I Do With My Baby All Day?!* should be given to every peri-natal person as they give birth to themselves as a parent!"
—Paige Bellenbaum, LCSW, founding director, The Motherhood Center

"With tenderness and care, Vered Benhorin helps new parents find their grounding with activities and suggestions to help connect to their infants in loving ways. She reminds parents that humor is needed. Connecting through these loving games and songs and more is part of having a joy-filled and secure relationship with your baby. Bubble Moments are a must-have for every new parent—a calm way to be with your baby."
—Tovah Klein, PhD, director, Barnard College Center for Toddler Development

What Do I Do with My Baby All Day?!

· · · · · · · · · · · · · ·

SIMPLE WAYS
TO HAVE THE BEST
FIRST YEAR TOGETHER

VERED BENHORIN, LCAT

Countryman Press

An Imprint of W. W. Norton & Company
Independent Publishers Since 1923

This book is a general information resource about how to create and nurture connections with your baby. It is not a substitute for individual professional counseling or advice. Each baby is unique, each baby develops at its own pace, and each parent's relationship with their baby will be different. No one can predict how your particular baby will respond to the activities suggested in this book. If your baby does not respond to any of the suggested activities, if you feel severely depressed, or if you have any other doubt or concern about your own or your child's physical or emotional health or well-being, consult your healthcare professional. Do not hesitate to seek emergency care for yourself if you think it may be needed.

The names of actual parents and babies described in this book have been changed, and some parents and babies are composites. Any URLs displayed in this book link or refer to websites that existed as of press time. The publisher is not responsible for, and should not be deemed to endorse or recommend, any website, app, or other content that it did not create. The author, also, is not responsible for any third-party material.

For information about permission to reproduce selections from this book, write to Permissions, Countryman Press, 500 Fifth Avenue, New York, NY 10110

For information about special discounts for bulk purchases, please contact W. W. Norton Special Sales at specialsales@wwnorton.com or 800-233-4830

Manufacturing by Lakeside Book Company
Book design by Chris Welch
Production manager: Devon Zahn

Countryman Press
www.countrymanpress.com

An imprint of W. W. Norton & Company, Inc.
500 Fifth Avenue, New York, NY 10110
www.wwnorton.com

978-1-68268-920-2

10 9 8 7 6 5 4 3 2 1

To my babies, who taught me how to be their parent.
To my parents, for whom I will always be their baby.

And to Tsuri, whose hug is my home.

CONTENTS

Introduction   9

PART 1. CREATING BUBBLE MOMENTS

1. Setting the Scene   21

2. Speaking Your Baby's Language   40

3. The Art of Listening   57

PART 2. THE SECRETS TO SOOTHING

4. The Beat of Your Baby   69

5. Your Power Tool   83

6. It's All About You   96

PART 3. THE PERFECT PASTIMES

7. Relax and Enjoy the Show 113

8. The Only Game You Need 128

9. Now You're Talking 145

PART 4. THE REMEDY TO ROUTINE

10. Sound Sleep Habits 175

11. Your Daily Groove 194

12. Your Magic Wands 215

Afterword: Our Bubble Moment 223

Acknowledgments 231

Notes 235

Index 247

INTRODUCTION

Hi there, Parent.

You've got a new baby! Congratulations on embarking on the most intense, joyous, and challenging task of your life. Believe me, I know what a radical shift it is. For me it changed the entire course of my career (more on that later).

But along with the heart-bursting love that you never imagined possible, you're probably exhausted. It's a miracle you even picked up a book! You barely have time to go to the bathroom let alone sit on the couch and read. But something grabbed you, and I'm glad it did.

Maybe it's the nagging feeling that something is a little off, that you could be feeling better as a parent, or that time with your baby could be more enjoyable sometimes. Maybe you imagined feeling more in control as a parent. You have wonderful moments with your baby, but you want more of them and fewer of the ones that bring you to tears. I get it.

This book is here to help you find more moments of delight with your baby throughout your day. It will help make diaper changing a little less monotonous and the witching hour a little less torturous. Oh, and it will also help you get more needed sleep and rest.

This book is *not* here to say that you need to be with your baby all the time or that you need to *want* to be with them all the time. As we'll discuss, that's neither possible nor beneficial. Rather, the goal of this book is to make the moments you *are* with your baby more meaningful, joyful, and healthy for you both.

If you can make that happen, you've set your baby up for a happy and gratifying life to come. You've also made sure that you don't go to sleep anxious that time is going by too fast. Your deep moments of connection will confirm that your relationship is just as it should be.

I know how important this is because of my work as a therapist to parents and my studies in clinical psychology and music therapy. But even more so I know it firsthand. When I had my first baby, I was the alpha mom who was convinced I could gracefully add my baby to the list of all the things I was already doing. Despite my infant demanding my time, my body, and especially my attention, I held on to my boundaries like a buoy out at sea.

Mind you, I thought I was doing fantastically. If you had told me I needed to read this book, I'd probably say, "I don't need a book. I have an amazing relationship with my baby! I enjoy him to the fullest! I know exactly what to do!" But at this point I know that I was missing a crucial element that took me years to learn and years to figure out how to teach.

It has to do with surrendering fully to the moment when you're *with* your baby and knowing how to maximize your time together so you can be guilt- and anxiety-free when you're not.

I remember sitting on the rug with my first, handing him a toy. From the outside, it probably looked like we were playing together.

But that's not how it felt. What I really wanted was escape. I wanted to be anywhere else but there.

Meanwhile, in the graduate psychology program I was taking during that time, the infant class taunted me: "In the first year, the baby and mother are in a bubble together," my professor proclaimed as she drew a circle around two smiley faces on the board. I rolled my eyes at the idyllic illustration. *There is no bubble, and most of the time I'm not smiling,* I thought.

Sure, there were moments when I'd feel a huge amount of joy when we were together, along with a growing adoration I'd never experienced before. But often when I was with him I wanted to be away, and when we were apart I yearned to be together. I wondered if he was bound to develop the psychological issues I was learning about in class.

But now, after 13 years of working with thousands of parents and having three babies of my own, I realize that my professor had it wrong. She drew a bubble around the parent and baby as if it was a *constant*. But that's impossible. We can't possibly spend every moment in baby bliss. Instead, we have *moments* of feeling like we're in a smiley bubble with our baby. And the more moments we have, the better off our baby, and we, are.

The times we're present and feel connected to our baby are what keep us going through one more bout of mastitis or another sleepless night. They're the mental snapshots that make us grin as we fall asleep. And like a car refueling, a moment of effective attentive connecting also allows us to *disconnect* and take the space we need.

For our baby, the moments in which we're present and responsive are essential to their well-being. Not only are we better at tending to their needs, but in those moments we teach them what they can expect from us in the relationship; whether we'll be attuned when they're feeling hungry, tired, curious, or frustrated, or will miss their cues and be unreliable.

In the exhaustion of parenting and the alluring distractions of our modern world, these moments can sometimes be hard to find. But both the baby and the parent crave meaningful touchpoints with each other. They help us feel like we know what we're doing, and they help the baby feel safe and supported so they're emboldened to explore the world further.

But how do you make those moments happen? And, more importantly, how do you release yourself of the paralyzing guilt when they don't?

That's exactly what I've spent the past 13 years helping parents do. I blend practical tools from music therapy with research from attachment theory to teach parents how to communicate with their baby, enjoy their baby, and develop a more gratifying relationship. When parents learn how to communicate with their baby through tone, rhythm, melody, and mindfulness, they find more moments of *joy*. As a result, the constant daily struggles feel worth it.

When you have more moments of connection, you:

✶ Feel more in sync with your baby, emotionally and
   even rhythmically
✶ Feel like you know what you're doing as a parent
✶ Soothe your baby more effectively
✶ Make your daily routine smoother and more fun
✶ Make bedtime more restful and consistent
✶ Turn play into activities you both enjoy
✶ Increase communication with your baby

The truth is, these tools are what I needed when I had my first baby. Movies made me believe I'd feel a deep and undeniable connection the minute my baby was born. But that's not how it went for me.

I had just given up on my rock star dream, was working in an addiction clinic as a music therapist, and was in a PhD program for clinical psychology. I was intent on keeping my career going strong while mothering. But parenting took me by surprise, as it does so many others. Despite being a musician, I barely sang a note to my baby, and despite being a therapist, I felt out of control and overwhelmed.

At first I approached my baby like a problem that needed to be solved. I was a doer, a student, a problem solver. I could handle this! I obsessed over the technical stuff—how many ounces he ate, how many minutes he slept, what stroller was the safest, which bottle was the best—and wasn't focused on what actually mattered: *connection*.

I remember one middle of the night when I was sitting on the bed in a daze, attached to a pump, milk stains on my shirt, my body feeling foreign, my mood defeated. Meanwhile, my husband gently held our baby and sang to him as they seemingly floated around the apartment. I stared at them, wondering how he had achieved the idyllic parenting image that I had imagined for myself.

It took months before I found my way into motherhood. I needed to recalibrate what I thought mothering would look like and pause for long enough to see who my baby was and what he needed from me. And then I gathered what I had learned from my studies along with my creative instincts, and together we forged a new path.

I had conversations with my baby using his sounds, learned how to use my voice as another way to hold him and soothe him, and developed our language of play. We cocreated a relationship that felt like a secret language between us. He responded immediately to my shift, and mothering began to feel easier and even enjoyable.

I started writing ditties about how I was feeling and what I imagined to be his experience. One of my first was about our Sunday mornings together. He seemed so content to have us there with him. Or maybe it was me who finally allowed myself to relax into my role as a mom. The lyrics were from his point of view:

I cross my legs at my ankles
and wait for a song
'Cause it's Sunday and I got
mommy and daddy all day long

The songs I wrote during that period turned into the first of three award-winning albums for families. I began integrating my skills and education to develop a curriculum that would help other parents find their key to parenthood as I had. The program was called Baby in Tune.

My goal for the classes was ambitious: I wanted parents to experience delight with their baby in the class itself and send them home with practical tools to use during the week. Beyond that, I hoped to create a space where parents would feel comfortable sharing feelings of guilt, shame, or doubt that might have arisen during the week. My studies had taught me that without untying some difficult emotional knots, parents wouldn't be available to connect with their baby.

What I came to realize in the classes was that other parents were similar to me—they had every intention of parenting "right" and doing what was best for their baby, but they were spread too thin, and that's only increased in the past few years. With so many parents working remotely, the lines have become confusingly blurred. Home has become a place to avoid your baby just as much as a place to connect to them.

The last thing you want to be told is that you need to spend *all* day "attached" to your baby and "present" with them. It's near impossible in the modern world anyway. Instead, you need actionable strategies to help you have meaningful *moments* of connection during your day that will set the foundation for your relationship for years to come.

Over the past 20 years, psychologists and scientists have agreed that building a secure attachment with your baby is crucial for the baby's well-being. The research is robust, and the parenting books, podcasts, and articles help spread the gospel. The good news is that, at this point, parents know *what* they need to strive for. The problem is they may not know *how* to actually do it.

Like in my classes, I'm hoping that you'll not only gain new tools to help you with your parenting but will also feel a little less alone in it all. Each chapter starts with a vignette from class to introduce you to the topic and bring you into class with all the other parents who feel like you—who struggle sometimes and revel in others, who have daily parenting wins and are also caught in the daily hustle. You'll hear the voices of parents I've worked with sharing their concerns, doubts, and insecurities. And like in Baby in Tune classes, we'll also talk about the work that's involved apart from the baby—on yourself.

This book is a practical guide that will teach you how to have joyful, meaningful, attachment-building moments with your baby through three-minute activities that instill calm, inspire playfulness, and encourage communication.

The book starts with some background in attachment theory and the importance of nurturing your connection with your baby. You'll learn what it means to create space with your baby within which you can feel present and open to learning about each other. We'll go into practical applications, such as how to soothe your baby when they're fussy, make bedtime more effective, strengthen routine, develop ways to play together, and increase communication and language.

The book is laid out in four sections, each focusing on a topic that is top of mind for parents of babies:

1. **Creating Bubble Moments.** In this section you'll learn the foundation for communication with your baby, the elements of your baby's language, how to truly listen to them, what Bubble

Moments are, and why they are so important for your connection with your baby.

2. **The Secrets to Soothing.** This section is all about something
you probably spend a lot of time doing—calming your baby. It
explains what makes for an effective soothing strategy and the
impact your own inner state has on your connection.

3. **The Perfect Pastimes.** Building your connection with your
baby means finding the joy in it. This chapter offers easy, fun,
and even relaxing activities to do between all the necessary tasks.

4. **The Remedy to Routine.** Your baby's day follows a cycle, more
or less: eating, playing, soothing, sleeping. This section is about
making those rote moments more enjoyable and smooth for
you both.

The activities in this book help you drop into the present moment
with your child, learn about each other, and create a strong and
gratifying bond. Through listening, singing, moving, and seeing
one another, you'll feel more in sync and guide each other through
all of the challenges you'll face in your first year together.

We all want to feel close, connected, and present with our children, but it doesn't always come so easily, especially at first. By
using these three-minute activities to create what I call "Bubble
Moments," we stop the world for just a moment to *be* with our
baby. It's during those special moments that our baby will teach us
how to be their parent; they'll learn who we are, and we'll develop
a unique way of relating.

Although it may seem like an easy task to have a few moments of
deep connection with your baby every day, I know that sometimes
it can be a tall order. It was hard for me. But I'm with you. Together
we'll talk about how to give your baby *enough* of what they need so
that you're not ridden with guilt about what you're not able to give.

Parents often say that my songs make them cry. I think it's
because they feel less alone in their deepest parenting insecurities

and yearnings when they hear them because I'm singing about how I felt. My goal with this book is to go even further so that you won't only feel supported emotionally but will fill your toolbox with practical ways to create a joyful and secure bond with your baby.

As annoying as it is to hear as you're covered in spit-up, your boobs are leaking, and your baby is seconds away from a DEFCON 1–level scream, what the old woman in the supermarket says is true: "It goes by so fast." This snippet of their life (and yours) will soon pass, and next thing you know, they'll have a backpack on their shoulder and you'll be sobbing as you scroll through their baby pictures.

Instead of being caught between the guilt of not being present enough with your baby and holding on to the anxiety and fear of missing out, use these tools to make the moments count. For three magical minutes, you'll step into the present moment with your baby and truly enjoy each other within these activities.

So what do you do with your baby all day? You make sure to have some quality Bubble Moments when you can—responding to and learning about your baby through them—so that you can also step out of that bubble and be something other than a parent, guilt-free.

PART 1

· · · · · · · · · · · ·

CREATING BUBBLE MOMENTS

1

Setting the Scene

IN THIS CHAPTER, YOU'LL LEARN WHAT BUBBLE
MOMENTS ARE AND HOW TO CREATE THE
SPACE TO MAKE THEM HAPPEN.

I t's the first meeting of our 10-week Baby in Tune class. While the caregivers peel layers off their babies, they timidly greet each other and compare the ages of their babies. One mom tells a harrowing story of how her stroller got caught in the slush of a Brooklyn sidewalk and almost tipped over. The others empathize and agree it was a rough walk over.

I smile at the group and introduce myself, pick up my guitar, and start with a warm-up song—"Good Morning My Love." As I sing I feel the group slowly shift from the outside world of chaos, traffic, and winter to the room and to each other.

I can see the anticipation in their eyes. They're excited to meet other parents and are sneaking glances at each other. After years of teaching groups and going through it myself, I know that they've probably been feeling lonely. Maybe they're hoping to find a friend to meet for coffee, or maybe they just want to meet other parents so they can find out if others have also been feeling frustrated, con-fused, and exhausted.

They're also hoping this hour will help them alleviate some of the heaviness they feel with their baby during the day. They had imagined the first year to be different, not as hard. Now they're wondering what they can do to enjoy it more.

We finish the song and I say:

"You've made it to class despite all the hitches you probably had along the way— changing your baby's diaper for the 14th time, feeding for longer than you expected, swapping clothes again because your baby spit up all over everything, battling the stroller and getting them in, hoping they'd nap or not nap on the way. You've made a Herculean effort to get here, and you did it."

Dear reader, you did it too. Sitting down to read *any* book when you have a baby is no small feat. You spend your day soothing, feeding, figuring out your baby's schedule, chasing naps, and cleaning in between. And yet, somehow, the laundry gets done, you and your baby get fed, and you even find time to call a friend or a family member. And on top of all that, you're reading a book on how to improve your parenting? Kudos.

Like the parents in the class, you may feel that taking care of a baby is way harder than you ever thought it would be. But you do it, and you even do it well.

Not only that, in between the shushing and feeding, you're building a new relationship with this little person, and you're doing a good job. OK, you might be fumbling a bit along the way, as we all do, but you got this.

And yet something may not feel completely right for you in your parenting, and I'm not referring to the fact that you desperately need a seven-hour stretch of sleep or someone to *please* come clean behind the couch and find that missing bottle.

I'm talking about that moment you have before going to sleep, when you find yourself wondering what you did all day. You know you were busy the entire time but can't think of any moments that really stand out for you. I'm also talking about periods when you find yourself so overwhelmed with conflicting emotions at once—guilt, adoration, resentment, unrest—that you zone out and disconnect from your baby and your own needs.

You seem to be searching for another way. You wonder, *Why do I feel like something is still missing?* And maybe you wonder, *Am I doing something wrong?* or perhaps even, *Why are there so few moments when I actually enjoy this?*

What's Missing

To figure this out, let's think back to the moments in which you felt happy and gratified with your baby. What were you doing?

Perhaps you were lying on the floor next to each other and your baby was cooing. Or maybe you suddenly locked eyes with your baby as they were eating and you smiled at each other. Or maybe you were giving them a bath and you noticed how much your baby loves when you pour water on their belly, and it was soothing for you both.

I wonder if the moments in which you feel more content as a parent are those in which you feel more *present* with your baby. Often, we can spend all day with our baby, but that doesn't mean we are truly *with* them.

As you read this, take a moment to consider what it means for you to be present with your baby. What does it look like? What are you doing? And how do you get to that place?

You probably have many moments like that, even if they can be fleeting. They happen when you do something to make your baby laugh and suddenly you forget about something that bothered you, or when you sing a song that soothes you both instead of thinking about the dishes in the sink.

I'm talking about the moments when you say to yourself, *I hope*

I remember this forever. Those are the ones that make the hardship of caring for a baby feel worth it. They're not necessarily the Instagrammable moments, full of smiles or laughs, although those are nice too. Rather, they're the moments in which you feel completely connected to your baby in a way you don't with anyone else. It might just be a quick gaze into each other's eyes.

I have a feeling that what's missing from your day, and the reason you're reading this book, is because you want *more* of those moments. You crave more connection with your baby. Not all the time, because you also need your space (a lot of it, and that's OK!), but enough to make you fall asleep with a smile, knowing you had a few attentive moments of relating deeply with your baby.

It's a natural desire. It's actually wired into our brains to need to connect in a meaningful way with our baby. And it's part of your baby's primal instinct to search for a deep attachment with you. It improves their short- and long-term well-being, and there's lots of research to back it up.

Connection Is Key: The Research

In the past 50 years, there's been a growing body of research called "attachment theory." It's one of the most studied areas in psychology today and teaches us what our babies need from us to thrive.

Attachment refers to the emotional bond we have with each other. John Bowlby was the first to conceive of the theory of attachment, and Mary Ainsworth brought his work to life in her lab research.[1]

At the time, theorists believed that babies attach to their caregivers primarily out of a survival mechanism driven by the need to feed. Bowlby disagreed; he believed that babies are driven by a *psychological need for nurturance, safety, and protection.* Turns out, he was right.

To test this, Ainsworth devised a research model, the Strange Situation, which set out to prove Bowlby's theory.[2] Her work changed the way we understand human nature. She noticed that babies' behaviors with their caregivers could be narrowed down and classified into three types of attachment styles (secure, insecure-avoidant, and insecure-ambivalent/resistant). These attachment styles pointed to the *quality* of the relationship between the baby and caregiver.

> Attachment theory teaches us a crucial lesson: *Connection* is most important to your baby's well-being.

Long-term studies that set out to investigate her findings more deeply revealed that those same attachment behaviors formed in infancy shape the types of relationships we have years later as well, into adulthood.

Attachment theory teaches us a crucial lesson—*connection is most important to your baby's well-being.* The bond you have with your baby impacts their cognitive, emotional, and social development and how they'll relate to others throughout their lives.

Secure Attachment

The healthiest form of Ainsworth's attachment styles is called "secure attachment." It refers to when babies feel they can consistently depend on their caregiver for emotional and physical support.

When the baby senses that their signals are responded to—that is, they're fed when hungry, soothed when distressed, put to bed when tired, smiled at when they smile, and picked up when they're uncomfortable—they develop the assurance that their caregiver will notice and provide what they need.

Here's the important part: When your baby can *depend* on you to be *responsive* to their needs, it gives them confidence to eventually, step by step, separate from you and explore the world. I hate to say it, but that's your job—to get your baby to the point where they can leave you and go out on their own (sob!). Having a secure attachment with you means they'll be ready to do so and will be able to make close and lasting relationships with others.

You want your baby to move through the world knowing how to ask for support from others when they need it. You also want them to learn how to soothe themselves one day when you're not there. You teach them how to do these things by responding to their distress and helping them regulate their emotions during these early years. Your baby learns not only how to do it themselves but that people around them can be helpful and reliable.

Your Baby's Home Base

In the ideal situation, you become like a home base for your baby. They're able to stray because they know home base is there when they need to get support and reassurance.

Here's a physical way of thinking about it: Have you ever seen your baby roll away or look away from you and then glance back? That glance is a quick check-in with home base (you), making sure you're still there. A few months later, they may crawl away, and when they feel they've gone too far, they'll come back into your arms, back to home base, to check in. Knowing you're there allows them to keep increasing the distance and time they're away. When they learn to walk, they'll venture into another room entirely and come back when they need comfort or simply glance at you across the room to make sure you're there.

And then one day they'll call from college and say, "Hi, Mom. Just checking in," which once again, will be their way to touch home base. As your baby grows, the invisible rubber band between you and your baby stretches farther and farther. But it's always there.

Home base is even more of an emotional concept. The more consistently responsive you are to your baby's distress by soothing them and helping them regulate their emotions, the more they learn that they can depend on you to keep them safe and to comfort them. For instance, when your baby cries and you pick them up, it not only soothes them but allows them to expect it the next time they're upset. Knowing you'll help them when they need it allows them to go out and take risks, climb the slide, or ask a new friend if they want to play. As your baby grows, they'll feel emboldened to do things that feel scary or challenging because they know they'll have emotional support if they need it.

When we're consistently responsive to our babies, they trust that we're a secure base from which they can stray, knowing they'll get the support they need upon return.

On the other hand, when the baby doesn't feel that the caregiver is available and dependable, and instead is inconsistent, unresponsive, or rejecting, they can feel apprehensive about venturing into the world, both physically and emotionally, and their behavior can be stunted.

Oh no! you might be thinking. *My baby may not have a secure attachment! Their growth may be stunted!* Before you spiral into parent insecurity land—and trust me, I've been there—keep in mind that you are already intuitively doing a lot of what we just talked about.

You're Already Doing It

If I were to set up a video camera in your home (as Daniel Stern, Colwyn Trevarthen, and Berry Brazelton all did in their work in the early 1970s), I'd see millions of micro-moments in which you're attuning to your baby without even realizing it.[3] Attachment behaviors often happen instinctually throughout your day.

The video would show how you intuitively mirror your baby's distraught expression when they whine, lowering your brow and

 saying, "What's wrong, baby?" Or how you suddenly lock eyes and smile at each other, each mimicking the other's delight, squinty eyes, and happy noises. Or how you instinctively pick up your baby when they cry and need soothing.

Although we do many of these attachment behaviors naturally, there are also times when we're too overwhelmed ourselves to respond, or when we're distracted or busy, and that's OK. Donald Winnicott, a psychoanalyst and pediatrician who was a contemporary of Bowlby's, coined the phrase "the good-enough mother."[4] His point was that, as the baby grows, it's natural for the parent *not* to adapt to the baby's needs all the time, and this can even be beneficial for the baby as they develop independence.

Meaning the "perfect" parent is actually *imperfect* and not present 100 percent of the time, and that's OK and normal. But the *quality* of your relationship with your baby (not necessarily the time spent) is imperative to your child's well-being and is the biggest indicator as to whether your baby will grow up to have a gratifying life surrounded by friends and family. No pressure!

In the modern world, with all of its distractions and expectations, misattunement happens more than we'd like it to.[5] Don't worry, most babies do develop a secure attachment. But there's a lot of room for growth and learning for all of us.

You're reading this book because you had a sense that your relationship with your baby could be deeper, healthier, and more joyful for you both. That applies to *all* of us. The trick is to develop the skills or exercise the muscles to make that happen. "The secret to secure attachment," writes Bethany Saltman, who penned a beautiful memoir about attachment, "is mutual delight."[6] This book is here to help you *both* delight in each other, making the moments you are with your baby count a whole lot.

Developing the Muscle

There is no one prescription or set of rules for how to improve your attachment with your baby. Contrary to what the latest parenting fads will have you think, it doesn't have to do with attachment parenting (the name was co-opted), wearing your baby in a sling, breastfeeding, co-sleeping, or any particular approach to parenting.

Instead, it has to do with being attuned and sensitive to your baby in the unique way they need you to be. It means responding *in the moment* to their needs. (This entails responding to your *own* needs, too, and being authentically *you*.) Responsive parenting doesn't happen at one particular moment but, rather, all throughout your day.

While there isn't one approach or method ensuring that you're developing a secure attachment with your baby, there are ways to strengthen your *attachment muscle*, or your ability to be more sensitive to your baby.

First and foremost, it has to do with becoming more aware of your own inner state and how that's reflected in your behavior. Beyond that, it's about developing the ability to really *listen* to your baby and communicate with them so you can understand what they need, learn who they are, and figure out what they prefer.

The activities in this book are a way to strengthen that muscle. As with any skill, the more practice and positive experience you have doing it, the more it will become internalized and habitual. And like any skill you try to master—playing guitar, surfing, or cooking— this is a lifelong task. But unlike those skills, there is a crucial time to start that makes all the difference for you and your baby. It's *now*.

The Attachment Muscle Gym

To build your attachment muscle, you'll need to create the emotional space to do it. Let's think of it as your "attachment gym." In this space you and your baby will connect deeply while also holding on to each one's separateness. That's an important ingredient to developing a healthy and secure attachment.

In 1971's *Playing and Reality*, Winnicott coins the phrase "potential space." In this space, he says, the mother and infant are neither separate from each other nor merged; they are in the space in between. It's within this space, he believes, that creativity and play can occur.

This is a pretty abstract notion, but stay with me for a minute. Imagine you just met someone new at a party. As we tend to do with people we don't trust yet, you're evaluating each other, trying to figure out how you're different and where you're similar. Maybe you're wondering if you're being judged and you don't feel completely at ease. In a situation like this, until something shifts, your separateness from each other is palpable. You don't feel comfortable to act freely, and you're not feeling especially playful or creative. This is *not* the kind of space Winnicott is referring to.

Now let's look at the other side of the spectrum. Remember my teacher who drew a bubble around the mama and baby and made it seem like parenting a baby is a constant state of bliss? I remember her saying something like: "In the first months, the mother and baby are merged in a happy bubble." That's right when I rolled my eyes. I did feel stuck to my baby, or merged, but that was because my baby often felt like a leech I couldn't tear off.

We might have looked happily connected from the outside, but I felt more resentfully fused. I lost a sense of who I was. I felt angry about not having time to myself and couldn't even remember what I'd do if I had it. That didn't make me a good partner for creating potential space with my baby where I'd feel creative and playful. I just wanted to create space *between* my baby and me. That's obviously not what Winnicott meant either.

Now think of your most connected moments with your baby. It's when you're both separate and merged. You don't come as Mother, as if it's a given condition with expected behaviors; rather, you allow your baby to show you how to be *their* mother. Maybe they elicit a playfulness and silliness that no one else in the world gets to see, or maybe you lock eyes and feel a different kind of focus than you've had with anyone else.

Your baby, in turn, learns how to be *your* child. They learn who you are, how to make you laugh, and how to respond to your inquisitive face in a way they only do with you. You have a unique meeting that could only happen between you both.

> You don't come as Mother, as if it's a given condition with expected behaviors; rather, you allow your baby to show you how to be their mother.

Creating the Space

To create a version of Winnicott's space, you need to make yourself available to your baby, both emotionally and physically, for a period of time. Physically, it might mean clearing an area to sit together on the floor, walking outside together, lying on your bed together, or sitting across from each other—any arrangement where you can readily have eye contact and hear each other's sounds.

Emotionally and mentally, it means shifting your focus to your baby without succumbing to outside distractions during those moments. It means being *present*. When you are, you're able to be receptive and sensitive to each other's subtle communication, which allows for *interaction* to happen. You're not expecting your baby to behave a certain way or putting demands on how you should parent. You allow each moment to unfold without rushing it or planning it.

Red Alert

Remember, we're not saying you should be in this space all the time. That's impossible. In fact, a necessary ingredient to creating this space is also having time *outside* it.

Maybe you're thinking, *Time outside baby land? Impossible! I don't have a minute to myself!* I get it. I lived it, and it took me a while to insist on my time away too. But even if you don't have physical time away from your baby, you can still have emotional breaks in which you allow yourself to put a pause on parenting.

Problems arise when we take space away half-heartedly or with guilt—then you're neither in nor out of the potential space with your baby but building resentment.

The activities in this book will help you create the space and work your attachment muscle *for a few minutes at a time*. That's it! And in those moments you'll learn more about who your baby is, who you are as a parent, and where your merging place is.

Bubble Moments

What I learned years after that day in my psychology class, through my own experience as a mother and a therapist, is that the bubble isn't a *static* condition. Rather, it occurs for *moments* at a time when you consciously turn your attention to connecting. I call them **Bubble Moments**.

When you're able to have Bubble Moments for even just three minutes at a time, you'll end your day feeling more gratified. Here's what Tricia, a mom in my class, said when talking about her day with her baby: "Sometimes I just want the day with my baby to be beautiful, but it's not. My daughter is hard at the witching hour, and we both fall apart. But I try to find at least a bit of time when we're both in a good mood, even if it's just a few minutes during the day. I go for small, happy moments, and I protect them and think about them when things get hard."

No Time for the Gym

Working parents often feel guilty that they don't spend enough time with their babies. They worry that they're not developing as strong a relationship as stay-at-home parents. They think that the parents who are home all day with their baby must be attentive and present with them all day.

Meanwhile, those who are home with their baby are developing their own load of guilt. They know very well that being with your baby is not the same as being *with* them. Despite being with their baby all day, they sometimes reach the evening wondering where the time went and what they even did with their baby.

Short periods of attentive time with your baby can make a huge difference in your day and your relationship.

The fact is that connecting to your baby doesn't have to do with *how much* time you spend with them; rather, it's *what you do* during that time that matters most. If you can accomplish the short, doable touchpoints in this book, they can make a huge difference in how you feel as a parent and your relationship with your baby.

Being Present

Let's go back to the class from the beginning of the chapter. Once we've sung our intro songs and have done a movement song, we're ready for the most important part of class—creating the space to be present with our babies. Here's what I say to the group:

"Now that we're here, what are we going to do with this time? We can simply sing songs, weave in and out of thoughts, look around, and enjoy being together. That's a lot and is very beneficial. But to get even more out of class, we need to fully *arrive* at this moment. We need to put aside our to-do lists, put our regrets and plans on the shelf, and *be* with our babies and ourselves."

So how do we do it, dear reader? The same way you can do it at home—by tuning into what you are feeling at this very moment. That takes shifting your focus to *sensation* and *breath*. In class, we do this by starting with a short breathing exercise and then doing a sensory activity (I'll explain exactly how those look in a minute).

The goal is to help you be present with your baby. All week long, you juggle responsibilities. You maintain your home and job while doing the infinite tasks that come with caring for a baby. You're reading this book so it can help you pause and create a space to *be* with your baby. The techniques here will help you stop and drop into Baby Time, where the clock moves slower and we're more aware of the possibility that each moment holds. When you meet your baby in this place, you can deepen your connection to each other, learn with curiosity, and not simply rush off to the next thing.

A Quick Warm-Up

Before we can create the space to have true connection with your baby, you may be in need of a reboot to calm your system. I've found that **Three Breaths** is a quick and easy way for busy parents to de-stress and get a happiness boost. It's taken from Buddhist practices and positive psychology techniques. Here's how we do it:

1. Breathe in deeply through your nose.
2. As you exhale, think of something you are *grateful* for.
3. Repeat three times.

That's it! It's so simple! But it has infinite benefits.

Research shows that recounting something you feel grateful for on a daily basis can make you happier, improve your health, increase positive emotions, build stronger relationships, and help you deal with adversity.[7] That's a lot! And during this time, when you're more fragile due to lack of sleep, possible hormone fluctuations, and no time to yourself, it's worth doing this simple practice that's been shown to do so much. And what happens when you combine that with breath? Taking in deep breaths slows the heartbeat, lowers or stabilizes blood pressure, and lowers stress.

Three Breaths Exercise

✶ Take in three deep breaths through your nose.
✶ Exhale out of the mouth, and as you do, think of something you're grateful for.

Tips for Success

1. **When you breathe, see if you can take in unobstructed, deep breaths into your belly, not just your chest.** As you exhale, you may feel a slight shiver. That means you're allowing yourself to fully absorb the breath and the emotion that comes with gratitude.
2. **Try not to plan what you're grateful for on the inhale.** Let it come to you as you exhale. You might be surprised by what comes up.

For instance, when I recently did this exercise, I was grateful for:

1. Writing this book.
2. My home.
3. My iced coffee.

You never know what it will be in that particular moment. Let the gratitude take you by surprise.

Now that you're more relaxed after an exercise that lasted just a few seconds, we're ready to have our first Bubble Moment.

Bubble Moment:
The Baby Buddha Massage

The **Baby Buddha Massage** is a way to join our babies and get into our *sensing* selves and out of our *thinking* selves. Luckily, you've got an expert to teach you how to do it. Your baby is your personal Buddha. They are utterly in the moment. They live fully through their senses, constantly exploring sensations around them through touch, smell, sound, and taste.

As you touch your baby, focus on the sensations you experience: the warmth of their bodies, the smoothness of their skin, their sounds, their smell, and even their taste. We help the babies feel their limbs, their fingers, their toes, their shoulders, their bellies.

To do this, you don't necessarily need a particular technique or to go to a baby massage class. You just need to have an open palm and gently move it across your baby's body while noticing their cues, telling you what they like and don't like.

In our class, we sing a song (often "You Are My Sunshine") while giving the babies a massage. This helps us relax even more, as slow music causes our blood pressure to drop and our breath to slow. Music also helps us focus, and in class our goal is to shift our attention to sensation and away from distracting thoughts. You might want to sing or play a song as you do your massage.

Here's why the Baby Buddha Massage is a great way to feel more present with your baby:

1. **Grounding through Senses.** Focusing on sensations, sounds, and smells is a way to stay attentive to what is happening right at this moment. When you do this, you're shifting your attention to what is in front of you and around you, just as your baby does.

2. **Experiencing Your Baby Fully.** You touch your baby all day—changing them, holding them, soothing them, but you probably often do it absentmindedly. Massaging your baby is a way to fully experience the physicality of your baby—their soft skin, small fingers and toes, pudgy thighs.

3. **Turning Off Thoughts.** Music and singing make us think less and feel more. When you move your hands over your baby to the rhythm of a song, you're letting your body lead instead of your thoughts.

After we're done with the **Baby Buddha Massage** and the **Three Breaths**, there is always a palpable shift in the group. Parents take deeper breaths, gaze at their baby with their full attention, and their baby returns the focus. They seem gratified to be with their baby in a meaningful way.

Those simple exercises help us enter a space where the parents are not caught up in their thoughts—judging themselves or others around them or overwhelmed with pesky "shoulds" or "shouldn'ts" because they're present to their *sensations*. They've distanced themselves from devices and have released some of their distracting thoughts. In this open and vulnerable state, anything can happen. Maybe even making a new best friend.

The space is created and the caregivers and babies meet each other within it.

In the next two chapters, we're going to dive further into how to create space with your baby in order to have more Bubble Moments, including how to speak your baby's language, what to look for, and how to attune to yourself and to your baby. But for now, let's recap.

Recap: HOW DO YOU CREATE SPACE WITH YOUR BABY?

1. **Limit Distractions.** Phones and computers are our biggest distractions (and addictions). They are so alluring! And they do such a great job of pulling us out of our baby slump when we want to be pulled out. And that's OK! But when you've decided to create space with your baby, it will help to physically distance yourself from devices. We're talking about three minutes. That's it.

2. **Come without Expectations.** The only way to let the moment unfold and surprise you is if you don't have expectations about how it should go. This means releasing expectations about who your baby is and what they should be doing, and also about who you should be and what you should be doing as a parent. Within the space, you will both create each other.

3. **Be in Your Senses.** Let your personal Baby Buddha show you how to experience solely through your senses: touch, smell, taste, sight, and sound. Focus on the sensations you are feeling. Music is a great aid to getting into your sensing self and out of your thinking self.

4. **Let Go of Your To-Do List.** Rest your thoughts about the future and the past on a mental shelf for a minute. You'll pick them back up when you're ready. And when you do, you'll return with renewed energy to get stuff done.

5. **Stay Curious and Notice.** This is another lesson from your little Buddha. We'll go deeper into this in the next chapter, but the idea is to be curious, ask questions about what is going on, what your baby is doing, what they're noticing, what their preferences are, and what they are exploring.

6. **Be Kind to Yourself.** When it's not easy to create space with your baby, that's OK. You'll do it later. Take care of your needs so that you can take care of your baby.

Bubble Moment: BABY BUDDHA

💜 Put on a song you like (or sing a song).

💜 Sway to the music so you start to quiet your thoughts.

💜 Hold your baby or rest them next to you.

💜 Run an open palm over their body. Feel the warmth of their skin, touch their fingers and toes, smell their head, taste them with your kisses, and listen to the sounds they make.

💜 For the duration of the song, try to stay in your senses, feeling your baby and the room you're in.

💜 For a song suggestion, try this one, called "One Day." We often sing it in the group when we're relaxing into the moment with the babies.

· · · · · ·
·   ·
(**2**)
·   ·
· · · · · ·

Speaking Your Baby's Language

IN THIS CHAPTER YOU'LL LEARN HOW TO
READ YOUR BABY'S CUES SO THAT YOU'LL
KNOW WHAT THEY NEED AND CAN AVOID
EXCESSIVE MELTDOWNS.

I't's our second class, and parents enter with some familiarity. Before we sing the "Hello" song, which incorporates the names of the babies, we go around and reintroduce ourselves. The caregivers each tell the story of how they came up with their baby's name. Some were inspired by family members, some by movies or books, and some just liked the sound of the name.

As the caregivers listen, they study each other without even meaning to. They instinctively pick up on each other's body language, facial expressions, and tone of voice. They gather information through nonverbal communication even more than through what's being said.

Meanwhile, the speaker does the same. She notices how her neighbor listens to her, whether their body language conveys interest and empathy, or if they seem distant or apathetic. Both sides intuitively evaluate how comfortable they feel in the presence of the other. They might not be conscious of it, but they're trying to figure out whether the person next to them might end up being their new best parent friend, and if they'll end up looking for day-cares together and vacationing with their families one day.

The parents may yearn for camaraderie, but their friend sensor is on high alert. If they feel even a hint of aversion from a parent or interpret a tone of voice or expression as critique, they may recoil and turn to someone else.

We all do this unconscious dance every time we interact with others. It's estimated that a whopping 66 percent of our communication with others is nonverbal![8] While we harp over our choice of words, our listener is busy decoding what we're *not* saying. It's the nonverbal cues that we use to determine whether another person is trustworthy and if they want to engage and cooperate with us.[9]

How does this relate to your baby? Because with your baby it's *all* the nonverbal stuff. Your baby's communication relies on three things—**face, body,** and **voice**—to understand you, and vice versa.

In the last chapter we talked about opening the space to have Bubble Moments. This chapter is about making connections by learning how to speak the same language.

> Your baby communicates through *face, body,* and *voice.*

Sometimes your baby's signals are easily understood—crying is a clear way for your baby to say, *Hey! I'm not OK right now!* Smiling or giggling is an obvious way for them to express pleasure. Often, though, your baby conveys *subtle* cues through their face, body, and voice that are harder to decipher. But if you learn how to do it, your life with your baby will get a whole lot easier.

Understanding the *Subtle* Cues

A mom in our class told us a story. She was out with her baby, having brunch with friends. For the first hour, her baby charmed the table. He smiled at everyone, waved, and even played happily in his stroller for 15 minutes. At some point he started dropping his toy and pacifier repeatedly. When they gave them back to him he'd throw them down again. The meals had only just arrived, and the parents were starving.

By the time they got home, the baby was fussy, rubbing his eyes, and flailing as they tried to change his diaper. Putting him down for a nap was torturous. It took 30 minutes of heavy rocking and holding to calm him down. Finally he fell asleep, and she and her husband collapsed into bed too. But 20 minutes later he was up again. Ugh!

Does this sound familiar? *All* parents know this scenario. It's what happens when we're not able to give our full attention to our baby's cues and then make up for it later. It's normal. These parents wanted to hang out with their friends and have brunch. But the more you become an expert in your baby's subtle cues, the better you'll be at catching them with even half an eye and responding in a way that may save you later.

The thing is, by the time your baby is crying, they've already turned a corner. They're not just *starting* to get tired, hungry, or overstimulated, they're already there. And the more escalated your baby gets, the harder it is to regulate them back to baseline. You know this; I don't even have to tell you. It's what happens on those challenging days when your baby is fussy but can't seem to be put to sleep or only sleeps for a 15-minute stint.

Before you find yourself crying to your own mother about how your baby just won't calm down no matter how much bouncing and shushing you do (or maybe that's just what I did), you can take some control and learn your baby's nonverbal language. When you understand your baby's subtle fussy cues, you can catch them before the meltdown of no return. And the more you understand their happy cues, the more often you can have those magical moments on the floor, the perfect song playing (maybe one of mine?) and your baby gazing at you as though you are life itself.[10]

The "What Could Be Bothering My Baby?" Game

It's 5 p.m. and your baby is fussy. You just fed them, so you know it's not that. You checked the diaper and it's dry. They took a fairly long nap, so they shouldn't be too tired. Earlier you both ventured out to a crowded sing-along. You wonder, *Is my baby overstimulated? Overwhelmed?* Or maybe the fussiness is unrelated. *Are they teething? Gassy? Do they have an earache?*

Sound familiar? It's the guessing game you play with your baby all day long. It can be so frustrating! Right when you feel like you're getting a handle on this parenting thing, your baby is inconsolable and you can't for the life of you figure out *why*.

But what you might not realize is that every time you play that guessing game you get a bit better at it.[11] In fact, maybe the other day you surprised yourself by knowing what was bothering your baby after just one glance.

Psychologists (led by Arietta Slade, my professor who turned me on to attachment theory) have a name for that super parent power you've been developing that often clues you in to what your baby needs (and sometimes fails you).[12] It's called **parental reflective functioning** (PRF).[13] PRF is the capacity to guess your baby's mental state from their behavior.[14]

Basically, parental reflective functioning is a fancy name for the important detective work that you do every day with your baby as you observe their behavior and infer or imagine how they might be feeling.

Here's what Amy said about her baby:

"My baby rubs her eyes sometimes. It used to mean that she was tired. I felt like I knew her cue and was proud of myself for knowing. But she's changed a little and now I think it might mean that she's had enough of whatever we're doing. Now when she does that

I pick her up and cuddle her for a while. Often she's ready to go to the next activity within a few minutes."

Amy felt like she had it figured out a month ago. But nothing in parenting is ever that simple, and our old tricks stop working at some point. Eventually Amy noticed that her baby's eye rubbing meant something different. Now it means her baby may need a change in scenery. How does she know? Because she did the guesswork.

Remember attachment theory from Chapter 1? Well, researchers found that whether a parent has a high capacity for reflective functioning is the most powerful predictor of a secure attachment with their baby. It makes sense—a secure attachment develops when a parent is responsive and attuned to the baby's needs. And attunement happens when a parent develops a capacity to understand their baby's feelings.

Interestingly, the ability to understand your baby's mental state is directly related to how you understand your *own* mental state and how it responds to your baby's. Meaning your ability to understand your baby's feelings and how they relate to their behavior goes hand in hand with understanding *your* own responses, thoughts, feelings, and behavior.

How Do You Develop This Parenting Superpower?

You don't need to get bitten by a radioactive spider to have the PRF superpower; it just takes some patience and energy. Here are three ways to develop it:

Be Curious. Continue speculating about your baby's state just as you've been doing. When you ask questions—*Why is my baby fussing after just waking? Is his stomach bothering him? Is he teething? Does he need to nap more? Does he need to be close to me? Is he feeling overwhelmed?*—it's not a sign of you being a clueless parent. Rather, it's a sign of you being a great parent! When you engage in compassionate trial and error to figure it out, you are exercising your PRF muscle and getting better at understanding your baby's mental state.

Reward Your "Mentalizing" Moments. Let's learn from a study that sought to help parents develop PRF.[15] Parents were videoed while interacting with their baby. Later they were shown small moments in which they had been *attuned* to their baby and were clearly "mentalizing," or working to understand their baby's feelings and thoughts. Just having these moments pointed out to them improved their PRF. The researchers found that it was more effective to show parents what they were doing *right* as opposed to critiquing moments in which they weren't as attuned to their baby.

You don't need a video to get you there (although how cool would it be to capture a simple day in your life with your baby, with *all* the successes and failures!). All you need is some self-reflection on your day.

Take a moment to think about it. Most likely you had some moments today in which you were *not* attuned to your baby—you were rushing to get somewhere, or were in conversation, or were washing dishes. But you also had many moments in which you *were*. How did they look? What was your baby doing? What were you doing? Those are a huge win! Congratulate yourself for your successful PRF.

Reflect on Your Mental State. Imagine this scenario: You're hanging out with your baby and get a disturbing call that pulls you out of baby/mama land. Maybe your friend is having a hard time with her partner and needs to talk. Meanwhile, your baby is getting hungry. By the time you get off the phone with your friend, your baby's distress has escalated to full-blown crying. That's OK! It happens. Your job in these moments is not necessarily to keep these situations from happening—they're part of being human, after all—but, rather, to become *aware* of your own mental state and how it may be affecting your baby's.

It can be exhausting to constantly run through a huge checklist of why your baby might be fussy. But it may help to know that most of the time, especially in the first year, your baby's distress will be caused by one of the big three: They're either **hungry, tired, or overstimulated.**

Actually, those three reasons often apply to older kids too. Learning their subtle cues now will help you be a better parent to them for years to come. Here's an example: When my eldest was a baby and he started to feel tired or overstimulated, he'd seem fine for a while and then suddenly he'd wave his arms and let out a whine and then go back to being quiet for a minute. He still does a version of that now sometimes, and he's 14! When my daughter was a baby she'd kick her legs wildly when she got tired. She's still known to run around and even kick when she's reached her limit, even at eight years old.

Cues from the "Average" Baby

You don't have an average baby. Nobody does. Every baby is different, and your baby's cues are unique to who they are.

Not only that, your baby's behavior depends on who *you* are. Your baby is smart, and their attachment mechanism is strong and adaptive. With time, your baby learns which behaviors elicit the reaction they need from you and which may even repel you.[16]

That said, there are some behaviors that tend to show up more often than others. Dr. T. Berry Brazelton, a pediatric researcher who developed a newborn assessment tool in the 1970s that is still used today, shifted the focus from screening for abnormalities the infant may have to discovering their strengths.[17]

He pointed out that babies are born with the ability to

communicate their needs and self-regulate. When a newborn cries, they are sending a message to their caregiver that they are experiencing discomfort. When an infant sucks—on their fingers, their own lips, or a nipple—they're calming their system by self-regulating.

Hidden behind your baby's subtle fussy cues is your baby's desire to communicate and self-regulate.

The subtle fussy cues below are examples of how your baby's behavior might be communicating more than you're aware. This list may jog your memory about your baby's unique behaviors and awaken your own observational powers so you can detect your baby's particular cues. Your job is to add **your baby's unique cues** to the list.

As you're thinking about cues, it's helpful to keep in mind the three elements of communication that your baby uses: face, body, voice.

Subtle Fussy Cues You Might Notice

Your baby might be communicating they are tired or overstimulated if they exhibit these behaviors:

FACE

Avoiding Eye-to-Eye Gaze. Have you noticed that sometimes your baby maintains eye contact with you for a while, while other times they look anywhere but at you? This behavior is more meaningful than you might think.

Imagine yourself meeting a friend for breakfast—you're both alert, looking into each other's eyes, and feeling connected. Now imagine yourself after a long day at work or with your baby—your partner is telling you about their day, but you're looking down at the floor. You're tired, and direct eye contact demands too much energy.

Your baby is the same way. When they're tired they don't want to fully engage, so they avoid eye contact. The way they do that depends on their level of mobility. A 2-month-old might turn their head away, a 9-month-old might turn their body away, an 18-month-old might walk away (and a teenager might hide in their room).

Another reaction might be staring into space as this mom observed: "I notice that when my baby is tired she gazes into space. At first I thought she was interested in looking outside the window, but now I know that when she does that she's getting tired." (mom of Gigi)

Red Eyebrows. Many parents in our classes report that their baby's eyebrows get red when they are tired.

Lowering of Eyebrows. Like the classic caricatures of an angry person, your baby might also lower their eyebrows when they're getting uncomfortable or frustrated.

Jutting Out of Lip. Even a slight jutting out of the lower lip might be a sign of your baby feeling sad or emotionally overwhelmed. It's often the precursor to a full-blown cry.

BODY
Erratic/Jagged Movements of Arms or Legs. When your baby is tired, they may start to lose some control over their body movements and move their arms and legs in a more jagged and erratic way. As they get older and can manipulate toys on their own, they may drop objects more readily, swat them away, or throw them down.

Clinginess. Many parents report that their baby is more clingy when they're starting to get tired. They seek your lap, want to

be held, and use your body as a way to turn
away from the rest of the world. That's their
way of self-regulating, reducing stimulation, and
seeking safety.

Striking. Sometimes when babies are tired they tend to swing
their arms more erratically and can strike you. As they get older it
might even be intentional.

Gripping or Pinching. When your baby is tired or overstimulated, their fists may be more contracted. Adults sometimes do
that, too, when they're frustrated. In these moments your baby
might look for something to grasp—your skin, hair, or arm.

VOICE

Lower Pitch. When your baby is tired they may grunt or moan
more than usual and their voice might sound lower in tone. This
is similar to adults. Think of the tone of voice you might use to say
to your friend, "Ugh, I'm so tired." Most likely you brought your
voice down a few pitches from your normal speaking tone. Your
baby is the same way.

One dad said, "My baby sometimes goes from 0 to 100, so if I'm
not looking I may not catch it. But I've noticed that he lowers his
voice when he's getting tired. It's like babbling but lower."

Subtle Happy Cues
You May Notice

These cues may be your baby's way of showing you they're ready to interact and play.

FACE

Maintaining Eye Contact. When your baby is content and rested, they're more able to hold eye contact with you. Looking into someone's eyes demands full attention and energy to engage. When your baby is alert, your face and eyes will be their favorite point of focus.

Relaxed Facial Expression. When your baby is alert, their face will seem bright and calm; their eyes will be wide open.

BODY

Fluid Body Movements. Your baby's movements may be more fluid and less eratic when they are rested and content. They will be more able to focus on an activity for a longer period of time and manipulate a toy more easily.

Willingness to Explore and Play. When your baby is content, they'll feel more emboldened to try new things like crawling farther away, playing with toys in a new way, or experimenting with mobility.

VOICE

High-Pitched, Melodic Tone. You've probably heard it many times—it's the high-pitched coo or babble of a content baby. When your baby is alert, their voice will sound more high-pitched and melodic. (I'm not referring to crying, which will also be high-pitched.)

Bubble Moment: EYE SEE YOU

💙 Lie next to your baby when they're content and alert.

💙 Look into their eyes and maintain eye contact for a while.

💙 Try playing the staring contest. (Most likely you'll lose. Babies don't need to blink as often because their eyes are so clean.)

💙 Involve your hands and fingers—move them like a jellyfish or octopus in a hand dance. Make your movements fluid and interesting. See how long your baby stays focused on your movements.

💙 Point to different parts of your face and your baby's face as you maintain eye contact.

Ideal Times to Learn Your Baby's Cues

There are certain times during the day when your baby might show their unique subtle cues. Being aware of when to look out for them can help you spot them when they arise. Here are some ideal moments to learn more about your baby's behavior:

An Hour and a Half After They Wake up from Their Last Nap. Your baby probably wakes up with a lot of energy and is ready to play. After about an hour and a half of wake time, they might start to lose steam. *Before* your baby gets too tired is an ideal time to start gathering clues for how they behave when they're *starting* to get tired.

In a Crowded Place. Babies can easily feel overstimulated by a lot of people and new faces. So do we! The next time your baby is with new people, notice their behavior during and especially after spending time in a crowd. Do they show signs of social fatigue? Are their movements different?

Shortly After Waking Up. Understanding your baby's fussy cues means also knowing their happy cues. What are the subtle differences in their behavior when they're content/fed/alert as opposed to when they're slightly tired?

During Transitions. Transitions can be tough for all of us, and the same goes for your baby. Next time you're putting them into the bath or pulling them out, or are walking from inside the house to outside, notice your baby's subtle cues. Did anything change in their behavior? Voice? Face? Or maybe they're totally fine with the shift.

About 45 Minutes Before They Usually Go to Sleep at Night. Catching your baby as they're just starting to get tired will make your entire bedtime routine smoother. Once you cross into "very tired" territory, your baby will be much harder to soothe and put to sleep. Start looking for their signs of being tired 45 minutes before they normally go to sleep. Once you become an expert at picking up on your baby's bedtime cues, you can start the Wind-Down at that point. It might be much earlier than you think.

What Cues?

If you've been reading this thinking, *I have no idea what my baby's cues are,* that's OK. Learning who your baby is and how they express their needs takes time. In fact, this is one of those things you'll be doing forever with your child. Not only that, as your baby continues to grow, their needs and how they communicate them will change. But looking for those little quirks that your baby does to hint at their state can help you help them to regulate and transition.

Here's an example of how this extends into childhood. Two years ago my family took a long road trip across the United States. We'd stay in each place for about five days and then continue to a new destination. A few months in, I noticed that my daughter, six at that time, would be quick to tantrum on leaving day. Simple things like finding her shoes or her brother taking her toy would spark full-blown tantrums.

It took me a while to realize there was a pattern—it kept happening right before we left each house. Before that, I treated each meltdown as its own event. Sometimes I responded with compassion but often with impatience—her reactions seemed out of proportion to what had happened, and I had to focus on packing, preparing, etc.

Eventually I realized what was going on. Leaving each place was hard for her. After finally getting used to a place, we'd once again head into the unknown, where she'd have to acclimate to a new environment. Since I wasn't experiencing the same anxiety, it took me a while to get it. For me, packing up to leave for a new destination was exciting.

Once I connected the dots, I was able to detect her subtle cues leading up to the tantrums and support her. Even before we'd start to pack I would talk to her about where we were going next and ask her how she felt about leaving the current place.

When you're able to notice a pattern in how your baby requests soothing, or less stimulation, or feeding, or sleep, your days will seem a bit calmer and you'll feel more in control.

To set you up for success, let's go over some obstacles that may arise as you try to detect your baby's cues.

Obstacles to Noticing Subtle Cues

Your Own Needs. When your needs aren't being met, it's much harder to be sensitive to your baby's needs and how they communicate them. *Duh*, you're thinking. *But my needs are absolutely not met right now. Most of the time I don't even have time to eat.* Of course. When you're in survival mode, you're not going to be as great at detecting subtle cues. But have no fear. As you're able to sleep more, your Sherlock ability will increase.

Here's a story from one of my classes: One mom, whose baby was one of those miracle sleepers from day one, shared that when her baby got tired he'd pull at his ears and his eyebrows got red. Another mom said she had no idea what her baby's cues were. Her baby woke up every two hours during the night, so she spent much of their day chasing naps. The next week she showed up and said that, after talking about subtle cues and hearing about other babies' cues, she tried to look out for them more. She was surprised to see that her baby also got red eyebrows when he was tired.

This mom was not a bad detective or a bad mom. She was tired! But being in a class or reading a book like this can help you sharpen your observation skills.

Distraction. The phone, cleaning, work, friends, the laundry, watching shows. There are endless distractions that will take your attention away from your baby. That's OK. Your goal is to limit the distractions when you can, especially during those ideal times to spot cues.

Old Cues, New Cues. You figured out your baby's cues for being tired or overstimulated, but now they've changed completely after a few months. It's a bummer, but it's going to happen. Employ your detective work once again. This time you'll be quicker at figuring out the new cues.

Postpartum Depression/Baby Blues. When we're depressed our lens of our environment is distorted. For instance, research shows that mothers with postpartum depression rate facial expressions of babies as more negative than parents without depression.[18]

Their emotional state affects how they interpret their baby's emotional state.

Most women experience some degree of "baby blues" after giving birth (but for a shorter amount of time than those with postpartum depression). During those periods of weepiness, impatience, anxiety, and mood swings, we're less able to be sensitive to the subtle cues of our baby or anyone, and that's OK. Give yourself grace, have patience. Your observation skills will sharpen again soon.

But if you're feeling like you have more than baby blues and it continues for more than a couple of weeks, please seek help. Continued anxiety and depression can be harmful not only to you but to your baby, specifically because you may be missing out on many of their cues.[19]

Fussy Cues or Fussy Baby?

One of the hardest questions for researchers to parse regarding infants comes down to nature versus nurture. How much of your baby's behavior is due to temperament—the personality traits they were born with—and how much is due to external circumstances like how you parent or what their environment is like?

For instance, when your baby is fussy, do you sometimes wonder if they're simply a fussy baby? Perhaps it's not a cue at all but rather who they are?

To answer this question, pay attention to frequency. Your baby's fussy cues are unique to who they are because each baby has a different baseline. If your baby is naturally quick to startle, cries more often than other babies, or is often hard to soothe, then you know that by now and you've probably come up with many strategies to support your baby's sensitivities. If you're reading this and wondering—*does that include my baby?*—then it probably doesn't. You'd know.

When looking to spot your baby's subtle cues, look for behaviors that *stray* from how they normally behave most of the day and show up about three or four times a day when they're feeling discomfort.

It Goes Both Ways

Just as you're busy reading your baby's cues to understand them and deepen your bond, your baby is doing the same to you. Not only that, they are *good* at it. They're like born CIA agents skilled at picking up on your most subtle expressions. They're reading how your voice changes slightly when you're tired or agitated and how your body language is more stiff or less inviting when you're overwhelmed. We'll talk more about how to listen to your baby and how they listen to you in the next chapter. For now, let's have a detective Bubble Moment.

Bubble Moment: BEDTIME CLUES

- About 45 minutes before your baby normally goes to sleep, you're ready to pack it in yourself. But twice a week, leave the dishes in the sink and put on your scientist/detective hat.
- Watch your baby carefully with your eyes, ears, and heart.
- What are they doing with their legs, arms, and head?
- How does their voice sound?
- Are they seeking eye contact or avoiding it?
- Are their movements fluid or jagged?
- How is their expression? Is there any redness or changes in how their resting face normally looks?

3

The Art of Listening

IN THIS CHAPTER, YOU'LL LEARN WHAT IT
TAKES TO TRULY LISTEN TO YOUR BABY IN
ORDER TO BETTER UNDERSTAND THEM.
DEEP UNDERSTANDING WILL HELP YOU
RESPOND EFFECTIVELY.

It's our third meeting of class and it's a turning point. At this point, caregivers aren't just sharing how many minutes their babies napped or how many ounces they ate but how it's all making them *feel*. Alicia says:

"I'm so tired today. This week there were days that Connor cried for three hours straight starting around 5 p.m. I just couldn't soothe him no matter what I did. I had to walk outside a few times just to quiet my mind and catch my breath. I just felt like—I'm not sure I'm doing this right."

The group is doing its job. Parents are feeling reassured that they can share their deepest fears without feeling judged by others. They're recognizing that they're not alone.

For me it's a pivotal moment as well. It means I have a green light to help the parents dig a bit deeper into their stories and uncover emotions they themselves might not even be aware of.

The question is how best to do this. The answer is the same for better understanding your baby.

It Comes Down
to Listening

When we're in conversation with someone—for instance, sharing a story about something that happened during our day—we don't always explicitly convey the underlying emotion. That's not because we're trying to hide it. Rather, most of the time we're not fully in touch with it ourselves.

But in class the goal is not just to have surface chat—we all have enough of that—but to help each other untie internal emotional knots. Hopefully the caregivers will go home feeling a little lighter and breathing a little more deeply.

To do that, they need to feel OK to share their deepest insecurities and anxieties, and to process them with the group. And when are we moved to open up to someone?

When we feel that they are truly *listening*.

Listening deeply is a skill. Some may have a proclivity toward it, especially if they grew up taking the role of caretaker for others. But for everyone, this skill can be developed and honed. The reward is immense. When we're able to listen fully, we open ourselves to deeper connection with others and to expanding our own experience of the world.

Getting to the Bottom
of a Feeling

In class we try to turn on our deep listening skills with each other as well as with the babies. But it takes some work. Here's an example. A mom in class said this: "My baby woke up a few times during the night. By the time it was morning I was so tired and had to hand the baby to my husband, who was getting ready for work. I wish I didn't have to do that. I felt like I should have been able to take care of the baby myself."

When you read this, you might feel like you understand what this mom was talking about and how she might have been feeling because you can relate it to your own personal experience.

Maybe your first response would be to encourage the mom that she had every right to hand the baby to her husband, who should have been sharing the load. Or maybe you would empathize with her feeling of incompetence and would recognize your own fantasy of what a "good" mom should have been able to do in hers.

The fact is that we don't know exactly what this mom felt from this snippet above. Any speculations would be born out of our own assumptions. That's natural. We're all prone to fill in the gaps.

But to listen deeply we need to press **pause** on the instinct to assume we know how someone else is feeling and **ask questions**.

Questions help us gather new details and fill in blank spots we may have. Here's how that might look with this mom.

Instead of reacting right away, I might **pause**. And then, like an investigator trying to gather details to paint a clearer picture, **question**.

ME: "Can you remember what you were doing when you gave your husband the baby?"

MOM MIGHT ANSWER: "I was sitting on the chair feeding my baby, but my eyes kept closing. For a second I actually thought I might drop the baby."

Now that the mom is remembering that moment she may be able to pinpoint how she *felt*.

ME: "And how did that feel?"

MOM: "It was scary. I felt like I couldn't trust myself to care for him that morning."

That's very different from the assumptions we might have had earlier. In this case, it wasn't shame or anger but *fear* she felt. She had reached her limit and needed help at all costs.

Another scenario might have looked like this:

MOM: "It felt frustrating. I don't understand why I can't get my baby to sleep through the night. It seems like other babies sleep so easily. I feel like I'm doing something wrong."

This is a different story. Here the mom is talking about the "I'm not a good parent" shame that we all feel sometimes.

Other possible answers could have led to so many other directions—discontent with her relationship with her partner, frustration or shame that she is not working (and her husband is), etc.

So how can you develop and apply this skill with your baby, and really with everyone in your life, so that you can deepen your relationship with them?

Baby Listening 101

With adults, we question. But since you can't *ask* your baby for details, you'll have to gather them through close **observation.**

Knowing how to respond to your baby gets increasingly complicated as they grow. In the first weeks it's fairly simple. They're learning how to adapt to the outside world—how to eat, sleep, poop, and be a separate being. In those weeks your baby needs you physically close. Their fussing can usually be soothed by feeding and holding.

With your baby, the two elements of listening are pause and observe.

But after that, knowing *when* to respond and *how* to respond gets increasingly complicated. For instance, when your baby starts fussing you might be immediately moved to feed them. It's a fix that always works because it provides not only food but also your hug and a cozy place to sleep. But was your baby actually hungry at that moment?

It May Not Be What You Think

There are times during your day with your baby when it's clear that a response is needed. For instance, when your baby is hurt or distressed they need immediate soothing or care.

However, there are so many more moments in which an immediate response isn't clearly called for. In those moments it might be a good idea to pause and observe to better figure out what your baby needs from you at that moment.

Here are some examples.

FIRST WHINE

Your baby is playing with a ball and suddenly starts whining a little. You look over and see that the ball rolled out of their reach.

Assumption: Your baby is whining because they can't reach the ball and they might not stop whining until they can.

Action Based on Assumption: You move the ball within reach of your baby.

Alternative: Pause, Observe: You don't react right away. You stop to see whether the complaint is momentary. Maybe your baby finds something else to occupy them.

HELPLESS GLANCE

Your baby is trying to do something challenging like stacking blocks. They've tried a few times and then look up at you.

Assumption: Your baby is frustrated and wants help.

Action Based on Assumption: You go over and gently show them how to do it.

Alternative: Pause, Observe: You look for another moment and maybe your baby goes back to trying. You realize they were looking at you as if to say, "This is so hard!" but weren't actually asking you to intervene.

QUESTIONABLE FALL

Your baby is crawling and hits their head on the table. Or they're walking and topple over, hitting a chair on the way. They immediately look over at you.

Assumption: You see the glance as conveying pain and asking you for help.

Action Based on Assumption: You go over and pick them up to soothe them.

Alternative: Pause, Observe: You stop for a moment to see what happens next. Your baby puts their hand to their head while looking at you. You respond with an empathizing look but wait to act. Maybe your baby turns away and continues crawling toward the toy they wanted.

With all these scenarios, if your baby's distress increases you'd probably soothe them.

But before you launch into action, you might pause a second and learn more about what your baby needs at that moment.

The more you do this, the more you'll learn the body language your baby uses when they absolutely need you—what facial expression or tone they use and how they behave when they might want to share an experience with you but aren't necessarily looking for your intervention.

When you observe before acting, you're teaching your baby important lessons:

- They can count on you to be there, understand them, and help if they need it.
- You are sensitive to what they need.
- You trust them to self-regulate when they can and call you when they can't.

What *Your* Baby Needs

Parents' responses can look very different from one baby to the next and in each situation. One of the most fascinating findings from the Strange Situation studies created by Mary Ainsworth was how different secure attachment can look for each baby/ parent duo.

In the Strange Situation study, babies are left in a room with a researcher whom they don't know, as well as being left completely alone for a couple of minutes. But how the baby reacts to those stressful situations is less important to the researchers. They are more focused on what happens next, when the parents return to the room.

The babies who are securely attached seek contact in some way upon reunion with their parents. But that can look very different. Some babies just need a glance at their caregiver to gain reassurance, and some run over and need a hug to regulate. The manner in which the baby makes contact with home base is less about the quality of attachment and more about the baby's *temperament*.

You know your baby better than anyone. You know when they need you to hold them, be near to them, or simply give them an empathizing glance. Once you've paused and observed, you can rely on your instinct to respond the way your baby needs.

Your Reactions Are Powerful

Without assessing the situation before acting, you run the risk of teaching your baby to need you when they might not. They might understand your reaction to mean your intervention was required and they couldn't resolve the issue on their own.

If you don't pause and observe, you run the risk of teaching your baby to need you when they might not.

Marsha's baby, Dylan, was fussy in class. She immediately pulled out strawberries and handed them to Dylan, who happily received them and began eating. Once he finished, he started rummaging in his mother's bag, looking for more snacks. When he didn't find any, he started whining once again.

Was Dylan originally fussing because he was hungry? It's possible. But maybe not. Perhaps he was sick of sitting, had gas, was bored, or was teething. Marsha's knee-jerk reaction to hand him food might have been a way to soothe orally. Adults reach for food all the time when they're anxious. And Marsha herself may have been feeling uneasy because her baby was fussy in class. That's natural. But when possible, taking a minute to assess and tune out your surroundings can help you make more productive decisions.

The researcher and author Brené Brown often uses a quote she attributes to Viktor Frankl about the pause before response that I'm referring to: "Between stimulus and response there is a space. In that space is our power to choose our response. In our response lies our growth and freedom."[20]

In our baby world, Frankl's stimulus would be your baby's bid for attention, and the response is your reaction. If you are careful to allow space between them and disentangle the two, you'll have more freedom to mindfully choose how to behave and avoid creating habits that are not beneficial to your baby (or you).

Maybe It's Not Good or Bad, It Just *Is*

Your baby is probably more Buddha-like than you are. While adults often assign positive or negative value to experiences, babies simply accept the world around them *as is*, without judgment.

Here's an example: A dad told a story that he was sitting on the floor, playing with his baby. Together they patiently built a tower out of blocks. It took a while because the baby was only just learning how to place a block gently on top of another block. Shortly after they had placed the last block on top, the dog walked through the living room and his tail knocked over the tower.

The dad immediately said, "Oh no! The tower fell down!" In class he expressed his own frustration and described his baby staring at the blocks. As he told the story, he realized his baby might not have seen the event as negative. He might have just been curious about it, watching the blocks fall down and scatter.

Once again, taking a moment to pause and observe can allow you to take your baby's lead and react as they do—often with curiosity rather than judgment.

. . . .

Recap: HOW TO LISTEN TO YOUR BABY

1. **Pause.** There is no need to respond immediately. Take a breath.
2. **Ask Questions by Observing.** What is my baby experiencing? What might they be feeling? Is this my own need or theirs? If you don't know, that's OK. Give yourself more time to figure it out.

3. **Don't Assume.** Your baby may not have the same emotional reactions you have. Before you assume they're feeling a certain way, observe some more. When a ball rolls away, they might watch it intently because they're interested in the physics of it—will it roll back? They might not be as interested in the possession of it as we may think.

4. **Check Your State.** How are you feeling at that moment? Perhaps you're more on edge than usual. If so, you might have less tolerance for triggers that your baby can handle. The only way to deal with this one is to do work on your own responses to stress. That means going to therapy, talking to friends, figuring out your patterns of behavior.

After you've listened, go ahead and:

1. **Empathize.** If you feel that you've paused and observed and have a good idea of what your baby needs from you, respond with all your heart. Show them you understand how they feel. Tell them what you think they might be feeling.

2. **Respond Appropriately to Your Baby's Needs.** Do what you feel your baby needs in that moment—help, a cuddle, food, etc.

Bubble Moment: THE PAUSE

💜 Take a few minutes during feeding or playing to try this.

💜 Wait until something happens that makes you have a knee-jerk reaction—the fork falls, the toy rolls away, the tower topples, banana slips, etc.

💜 Instead of reacting immediately, take a pause.

💜 Look at your baby and assess how they respond.

💜 Do they seem to have a strong feeling about it? Are they looking to you to assign a value to it? Did they react in some way initially but feel less strongly after?

💜 If your baby is showing a strong reaction, empathize. Show them you understand how they're feeling. Soothe them physically and emotionally.

PART 2

THE SECRETS TO SOOTHING

4

The Beat of Your Baby

IN THIS CHAPTER YOU'LL LEARN RHYTHM
ACTIVITIES YOU CAN DO WITH YOUR BABY THAT
WILL BE BOTH FUN AND SOOTHING FOR THEM
AND THAT WILL INCREASE YOUR BONDING.

Our class feels a bit off today. We've just done the Three Breaths Exercise and are now doing the Baby Buddha Massage. The parents are smiling at their babies, trying to get into it, but I can feel the effort. Meanwhile, Lauren's baby, Naya, is getting increasingly fussy.

Lauren tries everything to soothe Naya—the pacifier, nursing, and distracting with the song. She looks apologetically at me. She glances at the door and I wonder if she's considering leaving.

I say something that I say in every round at some point because everyone needs to hear it: "We all have the 'fussy baby' sometimes. In fact, the fussy baby represents every baby out there just as the smiley one does. But it's really hard when it's *your* baby who's the fussy one. We feel embarrassed and out of control.

"But when it happens to you, what if you ignore the group for a minute and focus only on what your baby needs at that moment? Sometimes we need to tune out our surroundings in order to tune in to our baby."

Lauren's shoulders melt and she takes a sigh. Naya is still fussing, but Lauren seems a bit calmer. She stands up and picks up Naya. As the group continues to sing while seated, Lauren bounces Naya to the beat of the song.

After a few minutes (that I'm sure feel like hours to Lauren), Naya's cries turn into whines and then peter out. Lauren remains standing as the group transitions into discussion. By the time she sits back down, Naya is sound asleep. Lauren takes a sigh and tells us how her week was.

There's no way around it. Babies need an extraordinary amount of soothing in their first years. As newborns, their bodies are simply getting used to being outside the womb. Their stomach is adjusting, their lungs are getting stronger, and their skin is getting acquainted with touch. During those months, your baby is mostly saying, "Help me! I'm uncomfortable."

After several months, their experience becomes more complex, and although they may not have as much reflux, they're flooded with new emotions and sensations. Once again, they need plenty of soothing. They seem to be saying: "Help! I feel a lot!"

This comes as no surprise, I'm sure. You probably spend most of your day soothing your baby by bouncing on the bouncy ball, carrying them around the house, or rocking with them in the stroller or a rocking chair. That's why this entire section is devoted to that favorite pastime.

You often hold your baby in your arms and can see the calming effect your warm touch has on them. Studies show that the amount of skin-to-skin contact ("kangaroo care") a baby receives can impact their hormones and have a lasting effect, even into adulthood.[21]

But what about the rocking and bouncing? Why does that help your baby so much and why do parents seem to do it intuitively? That's what we're going to explore in this chapter—why *rhythm* and moving to a beat are so good for your baby.

The Rhythm of the Womb

Lauren's instinct to bounce her baby while standing was a good one. It's probably a dance you do with your baby multiple times a day. There's a reason for that. Your baby loves it! It reminds them of the good ol' days in the warm and comfy womb. As a fetus they were rocked to the rhythm of your steps, and their soundtrack was the consistent metronome-like sound of your heartbeat.

Not only that, at times they even synchronized their heartbeat to yours in the womb. In one fascinating study, mothers were told to breathe to the rhythm of a clock that was set to certain intervals. Their fetus sensed the rhythmical shift in the mother's heartbeat and synchronized with it.[22] Wow! Your fetus was rocking to your rhythm even before they were in your arms.

Once out of the womb, your newborn still yearns for a familiar rhythm and prefers to hear the sound of a heartbeat over speech.[23] In fact, a study shows that they even sleep more and cry less when they do.[24]

Not surprisingly, evidence suggests that your baby's tempo preference, meaning how fast or slow a rhythm is, is influenced by hearing your heartbeat in vitro and feeling the rhythm of your movements and steps.[25] That same preference continues. Even as adults we have a preference for patterns that resemble the tempo of the human heartbeat, and acoustic features of the womb are present in music from diverse cultures worldwide.[26],[27]

The tempo of your steps is not only preferred by your baby—most of the music we listen to and enjoy as adults is played to the rhythm of average steps. Basically, your baby is born with a beat in their body, and once they're in your arms it's hard not to notice how quickly they soothe when you walk, rock, or bounce.

Rocking to the Rhythm

"I'm not normally a big bouncer or rocker with my baby, but the other night I was amazed at how it worked. My baby was fussing in the middle of the night [and] instead of giving him the boob like I normally do, I sat in the rocking chair and held him and rocked back and forth. I couldn't believe it worked. Within minutes he was quiet, and I didn't even need to feed him. Oh, and the chair had a click to it that was making a rhythm for us both like a metronome."

Sarah's account of what happened with her baby may sound familiar, and there's science to prove it. Studies show that rhythmic rocking or bouncing decreases upper airway obstructions in infants and regulates respiratory patterns, which helps premature infants with scheduled feeds.[28],[29]

But wait. How do they know it was due to the rocking or bouncing? Maybe it was just the holding. Well, yes. Simply holding your baby regulates their nervous system and heartbeat.[30] But, when rocking a baby was compared with motionless holding, movement won and had the greatest soothing effect on the babies.[31]

The Missing Piece

OK, so bouncing or rocking can be soothing and regulating for babies, and we know that a consistent rhythm is also calming for them. But there's something missing.

Have you ever tried to dance without music? It's not so easy. You don't have a beat to groove to, and your body isn't feeling inspired to move. It's like trying to do a workout without music—you can do it, but you'll probably exercise for less time than you would have if you were listening to music, and you might not push yourself as hard.[32]

Same with your baby. To make your rhythmic movements not only more effective but more consistent, *music* is key.

Let's remember the goal of this book. It's not a sleep guide or a feeding manual, although the tools here can help with both. Rather, the goal here is to help you *enjoy* your baby. By the time you've finished reading this book, hopefully putting your baby to sleep or soothing your baby won't just be a task you need to get done, but a process you will delight in (or at least suffer through it a bit less). Music plays a big part in that.

Your baby responds to music from day one. It can help you soothe them, engage with them joyfully, and increase your connection.

Yes, you're dying to just get them down and collapse on the couch with a new episode of your favorite show. That's normal! You're exhausted. But if you can find ways to be more intentional and use tools that we know increase enjoyment (like mindfulness and music), you'll not only feel more satisfied as a parent but will actually be more effective in your parenting.

Music makes us happier. It reduces anxiety and depression while increasing endorphins and—most importantly for you and your baby—social connection.[33] No doubt you've experienced it in your life many times. Now let's see how it affects your baby.

Your Little Musician

As we mentioned before, your baby came out of the womb beatboxing to the rhythm of your heartbeat. Once out, they're even more Jay-Z than you think. Their ears are immediately clued into the structure of rhythm. In fact, babies as young as two days old can even tell when a downbeat is left out of a rhythm sequence.[34] You read that right— two days old! The ability to perceive beats is relatively rare among other species yet develops spontaneously among humans.

Babies are also able to detect inconsistencies in the rhythm of foreign music where you and I probably wouldn't be able to. In one study, six-month-old babies could sense variations in Balkan music, but North American adults could not. Presumably, the adults have already become accustomed to music from their culture and are not as sensitive to other rhythmic structures.

What happens to their music sensitivity as they grow? It's got a lot to do with you.

The Way You Move

The way you bounce and move while holding your baby plays an important role in how they experience and perceive music. Your movement teaches them the strong and weak beats in a rhythm, which will eventually help them move and dance in time with music.

Your baby is so clued in to how you move to a beat that it affects their preference. In one study, adults held their babies while bouncing. Some bounced every two beats (a march) and some every three (in a waltz). Infants listened longer to, meaning they preferred, the version that matched the pattern they were bounced in.[35]

Your movement to music affects how your baby perceives music.

This is fascinating because it means your baby can use movement-based information to help them understand a beat they hear.

Would the babies have liked the rhythm they were bounced to if they had just watched you move to the music but didn't move themselves? Nope. The researchers checked that. The babies needed to be rocked themselves to develop a preference.

Babies smile more when their involuntary movements align with music they're hearing.[36] And once they have control over their movements, they tend to move to the rhythm of the music. Have you noticed your baby breakdancing? If not, look closer.

Interestingly, it's not just your movements or music that inspire your baby's dancing; it's your speech. They tend to move their arms and legs more quickly when you speak faster.[37]

Why Dancing Feels So Good

Think about a moment when you were at a party or a bar, dancing with friends. How did it feel? If it felt good, why?

Most likely, there are two things that felt great: moving your body to the rhythm of a song and synchronizing your rhythm with others. We're social beings, and dancing is one of the ways we communicate with others.

In fact, the "dancing gene" has been passed down through generations because it was a survival mechanism. It helped with social interaction, obtaining a mate, and communicating with others.[38] Coordinating movements with others also helped to deter outside threats who might see a group moving together as much more powerful and dangerous.[39]

By eight months your baby can perceive when someone is a "bad" dancer, dancing out of sync with the music.[40] This is a big deal. It means your baby understands the idea of a recurring beat that can be anticipated as well as how movement can go with a beat.

I Like Your Groove

What does this all have to do with your relationship to your baby? Well, we know babies love a beat *and* love to bounce to the beat. Now comes the interesting part and what this book is all about: When you and your baby move together, it increases your *bond*.

It turns out that when babies move to a rhythm with someone else, they feel an affiliation with them. In a fascinating study, Researcher A holds a baby in a carrier facing outward and dances to the rhythm of music on the speakers.[41] Researcher B stands facing the baby. With some of the babies Researcher B bounces to the rhythm of the music along with Researcher A and the baby, and with others Researcher B dances out of sync, a bit faster or slower.

After the dancing, Researcher B (the one who was facing the baby) goes to play with the baby. During the play she intentionally drops something and pretends she can't reach it. What happens next is the surprising part: The babies with whom she had bounced in sync were *much more likely to help her and pick up the item she dropped.*

What? Why? How does dancing in sync with the baby affect their social behavior?

It turns out that being in sync with others rhythmically creates *bonds* and makes us feel closer to someone else. The babies were less likely to be helpful toward the researcher who hadn't bounced in sync with them.

The hypothesis is that the babies felt more similar to the researcher who had bounced in time with them, and that made them act in a more empathic way toward them.

The takeaway? Being social with someone else, helping them, feeling connected to them, is not just a function of personality and experience. Rather, it's *feeling in sync* with them.

> Feeling connected with someone is not just a function of personality and experience. Rather, it's *in sync* with them.

Synchronous movement is a language of its own. It can guide our behavior without us even being aware of it. We feel this phenomenon all the time when we dance with people. There's a feeling of closeness with someone who boogied down with you to the same song.

The Beat of Bonding

Now let's think about you and your baby. When you move in time with your baby—clapping, bouncing, dancing, singing—it helps you build your bond with them. Your baby is constantly gathering information to help them understand your relationship. Being rhythmically in sync with them helps your baby feel not only physically close but emotionally close.

When you sing to your baby, their engagement with you becomes synchronized with the beat of your singing. In one study, babies who watched a video of someone singing looked at the eyes of the singer in synchronicity with the rhythm of the song![42] Researchers call this "entrainment": synchronizing brainwave activity to a stimulus or to others. It turns out that singing to your baby entrains rich social-communicative engagement, and that's exactly what we're looking for.

These days, more research is emerging that shows how music induces entrainment with others. When you go see a music show, your brain activity is entraining not only with the performer but with other members of the audience.[43] Meanwhile, the musicians are also entraining with each other.[44]

Here's a real-life example that brought this concept to life for me. It happened at the subway station in Times Square:

It was rush hour, and everyone was on a mission to get to work. Typical of New Yorkers, each was walking headstrong in their path, prepared to trample poor tourists who were meandering and looking at subway maps.

I was the same way. Running late, I needed to beeline my way through the chaotic crowd. But everyone was walking in different rhythms, and people were bumping into each other as they tried to pass each other. I was sweating with frustration.

Then I heard a distant beat. Someone was drumming farther down in the tunnel. As I kept walking, the sound got closer. From afar I could see it was a teenager going to town on four plastic buckets. His rhythm was infectious.

And then I noticed something that's stayed with me since. As the crowd around me and I approached him, we weren't bumping into each other anymore. People didn't seem as annoyed. In fact, we each had room around us, as if we were distributed more evenly in the small space. I wondered why that was until I noticed we were all walking to the beat of his drumming without even realizing it.

Rhythm organizes us and increases our bond.

While we were in earshot of the music, we were all cooperating, in sync. Then, as we passed him and the sound of the drums slowly faded, once again we hit entropy and everyone was walking "to the beat of their own drum."

How to Effectively Soothe Your Baby through Rhythm

Now let's get back to how to use rhythm with your baby. Here are two techniques that can be very effective for soothing and calming your baby. It's a good idea to give them both a try and see what works for you.

SOOTHING METHOD #1:
BOUNCE TO THE RHYTHM OF A SONG

This one might seem obvious, but I've found that parents need to be reminded. Imagine this scenario: It's 3 a.m. and your baby woke up crying. You roll out of bed, shuffle over to the crib, and pick up your baby, praying you can get them down as soon as possible. You know they're not hungry because they recently ate, so you bounce a bit, hoping that will work. It doesn't. You start singing "Twinkle, Twinkle, Little Star" softly while bouncing absentmindedly.

Now think back—were you bouncing to the beat of your singing? Often, we bounce faster than the rhythm of the song we're singing because our body is saying, *Let's get this over with, I want to go to sleep.* And of course, your baby feels that.

Next time you're bouncing or rocking your baby, put a song on or sing while you do it and make sure you're bouncing to the rhythm of the song. See if your baby soothes more quickly. I have a feeling they might.

Here are two good reasons to bounce in sync with a song:

1. **It soothes your baby more effectively.**
2. **It increases your stamina.** Although soothing at 3 a.m. is torture, bouncing to the rhythm of a song makes it a bit more enjoyable, which means you'll be able to soothe for longer.

Bubble Moment: SOOTHING

💜 Hold your baby in your arms or in a sling.

💜 Bounce them to the rhythm of a song you are listening to, a song you're singing, vocalizations, or even your breath.

*Note: This seems like a no-brainer, but when you soothe your baby in the middle of the night or in public, you might not be syncing your bounces with your sounds.

SOOTHING METHOD #2: TAP A BEAT

This one is surprising. You probably wouldn't assume that drumming can soothe your baby. But for babies about eight months and older, tapping and creating a steady rhythm can regulate your baby and help them feel calmer.

Here's how to do it: Start tapping your hands on your thighs at a steady beat. After a while, move to claps for about eight beats, then to snaps, then cluck your tongue, then tap on the floor. If your baby is still engaged, do the whole sequence over again.

I've seen this technique work over and over with babies in class. We'll be having a chaotic moment where some of the babies are exploring, some are starting to get tired, and some are playing with toys. The minute we start tapping the babies quiet down and look up with interest. They stay engaged throughout the entire three-minute activity as we move from thighs, to claps, to snaps, etc. By the time we're done with the rhythm activity there is a calmer feeling in the class.

And it doesn't just work with babies. Here's a story I'll never forget about the power of rhythm with others to soothe:

Before I started Baby in Tune, I worked as a music therapist on a psychiatric unit at Bellevue. One day I arrived to work and the nurses told me to prepare myself—the unit was particularly chaotic that day. I could sense it the minute I walked in. Patients were yelling in the corridors and there was a feeling of unrest. The nurses wished me luck as I walked to the music room. The subtext of their message was clear: You're going to need it.

I set up all the drums in a circle and opened the door to the patients. They entered with raucous voices and high energy. Once everyone was seated, I started hitting the conga with a strong and steady beat, using the lower part of my palm so it would sound resonant and deep. The patients each picked up a drum and started to play along. At first it was messy. It seemed like the patients weren't listening to each other but instead were hitting the drum to whatever beat they felt.

I started striking my drum more powerfully, hoping the sound would permeate the noise. I wanted it to feel like the foundation of a building that could hold us all within it. One or two started to play with me in rhythm. We continued on. Slowly, others joined us. I dared not syncopate the rhythm or play anything fancy. I just held down the simple rhythm with patience.

Eventually, almost everyone was playing together in a synchronized manner. We played for about 10 minutes straight that day. No talking, no singing, just filling the room with a cooperative beat.

After we finished we all sat still. The room felt different, calmer. In fact, the whole unit felt quieter. They silently filed out of the room while I put the instruments away. As I walked off the unit I noticed that people were talking in the hallway with hushed voices. Others were sitting quietly.

As I passed the nurses station, they looked up and smiled at me. "Thank you," one nurse said. "We all needed that."

Bubble Moment: TAP A BEAT

- Clap to a beat—one, two, three, four. Keep going for about four rounds (16 claps).
- Now move to tapping on your thighs for four rounds.
- Now snap for four rounds.
- Cluck your tongue.
- Tap on the floor.
- If your baby is still engaged, do the whole round again.

Want to take rhythm and drumming to another level for you and your baby? Go to a class!

Not to toot my own horn, but it turns out that taking your baby to a music class is hugely beneficial on many levels. Not only for soothing, as we've seen, but for your baby's language development. One study showed that babies who participated in a music class "showed superior development of prelinguistic communicative gestures and social behavior compared to infants assigned to the passive musical experience."[45] And while enhancing your baby's music acquisition and improving their social development, it's also a place for you to find your new best parent friend and feel less alone.

5

Your Power Tool

IN THIS CHAPTER YOU'LL LEARN HOW TO
USE YOUR VOICE AS A WAY TO HOLD YOUR
BABY, COMMUNICATE WITH THEM, AND
BOOST YOUR CONNECTION.

In today's class, Zoe, one of the moms, tells a story from her week. She says, "On Monday we went to visit my parents, who live an hour away. My husband couldn't join, so it was just me and the baby. I almost considered not going. I was nervous about driving with the baby alone there and back.

"The way there was easy because I timed it with her nap. The way back was hard. Mia started crying exactly when I was on the freeway. I couldn't pull over to feed her or reach for the bottle or pacifier. I knew we still had another 20 minutes before I could. I tried to reach for toys and throw them her way, and I held her hand from the front seat."

Sound familiar? We've all had these hellish drives where we're stuck on the highway with a crying baby and feel helpless. In this section we're talking about *soothing* and what might have helped Zoe on her drive.

What her baby wanted was to be held and taken out of the car seat. But there's another way to *hold* your baby that people don't often think about. It's your secret tool that can magnify the effect of your physical soothing and take its place when you aren't able to physically hold your baby. You know what it is? Your voice.

When I was in graduate school studying psychology, a professor told us about a toddler whose mother had brought her in for an evaluation. The mother explained that when her daughter was born, she had allodynia, a condition that caused her daughter to experience pain at the slightest touch to her skin. My professor, knowing how crucial physical soothing is for a baby's development, expected to see some sort of cognitive or emotional ramifications.

However, when he assessed the toddler, he found that she had developed normally on all accounts. He was perplexed. When he met with the mother again, he asked her, "What did you do? How did you help your baby develop normally despite her condition?"

Your secret tool is your *voice*. You don't only have your arms to hold your baby. You can use your voice as another pair of arms.

The mother answered, "I sang to her nonstop."

Here's how Zoe's story on the highway ended: "At some point I realized the only thing I could do was sing. During the first song she kept crying. But then I sang a song we love doing together. She always smiles when I sing it. After a couple rounds she quieted down and looked at me through the mirror. I couldn't believe it actually worked."

In both stories, the parents couldn't hold their baby to soothe them. Instead, they "held" their baby with their voice.

Your baby recognizes your voice even in the womb, and it has a calming effect on them. A study shows that fetuses can distinguish their own mother's voice from other female voices reading poetry.[46] Not only that, but your voice can help your baby's development. Research demonstrates that preterm infants who hear their mother's voice have better outcomes: Their autonomic stability increases and they experience more weight gain.[47]

And that's just in response to the baby hearing their mother *speaking*. Your voice is even more effective when you *sing*.

Studies show that babies remain calm for *twice* the amount of time when they hear a recording of someone *singing* as opposed to speaking.[48] In addition, singing to preterm infants has been shown to modulate the arousal of infants and lead to regulated heart rate and blood pressure.[49]

Your baby prefers to hear you sing rather than speak.

Now hold on. Did you just hear that voice inside your head? It said, *I can't sing! I can barely hold a note! This part of this book isn't for me!*

You're not alone. *Everyone* feels a certain amount of insecurity when they sing, including the thousands of parents I've taught. In fact, I would bet that all of your favorite famous singers would say they often feel insecure about their singing.

The reason we all feel vulnerable when we sing is that it holds more emotion than speaking. Singing bypasses our intellect and comes from a place of feeling. And that makes us feel exposed.

In addition, unfortunately, most of us have been told at some point in our lives to stop singing or that we don't have a good voice. Can you think of a moment when that happened to you? I can. It was in sixth grade, and I was trying out for a part in the play. As I was leaving the house, my mother said, "Since your voice isn't your strong suit, maybe you should add an interesting dance to your audition."

The fact that you're reading this book means that the buck stops here. You won't tell your child to stop singing (you might just tell them to go into the other room if you need some quiet).

Petra, a mom in one of my classes, shared that she was upset one day. She tried singing to her baby, but all she could hear was her internal voice telling her she wasn't a good singer. She called her father, crying, and said: "I'm not a good singer like you! I wish I could sing to my baby the way you sang to me when I was little. I always thought you should be famous. But I sound terrible."

He answered, "Baby, I can't hold a note. You and your sister always thought I could, but I'm actually a terrible singer." I get chills every time I think about that story. Petra remembered her father's singing as beautiful. It didn't make a difference how he actually sounded. What mattered was how she heard him. To her, he was a rock star.

> Your baby just wants to hear *you* sing. To them, you are a rock star.

Your baby wants to hear *you* singing more than Adele, Beyoncé, or Elton John. Yours is the voice that soothes them most. They don't care how you sound.

In the introduction, I talked about how I gave up on my rock star dreams when I got pregnant with my first. By the time he was born, my relationship to music was complicated and I didn't sing to him at all. Months went by while only my husband sang to him.

When I finally did, something was unlocked. My baby made me feel more like a rock star than all of the dark, beer-stinking venues I'd played in combined. When he gazed up at me with his big, blue eyes, it was clear that he enjoyed it so much, however I sounded. And while I soothed him, he soothed me. Together, we finally found each other.

When it comes to soothing your baby with your voice, I'm not talking about belting out a Lady Gaga song. In fact, I'm not even talking about singing a proper song with a verse and chorus. I'm talking about vocalizing and toning.

Vocalizing

In music therapy, there's a practice called **vocal toning** (developed in part by Diane Austin, one of my former professors) in which the therapist uses their voice, often by singing sustained notes, to support the client. They mirror or harmonize with improvised sounds and melodies. The technique has been shown to help clients feel calmer, more relaxed, and meditative.[50]

In some ways, vocal toning is similar to how a psychotherapist may repeat back what a client says as a way to show empathy and understanding. For instance, you might say to your therapist, "I'm feeling exhausted and overwhelmed, and I can't wash one more bottle." And your therapist might respond, "You're feeling exhausted and overwhelmed, and you can't wash one more bottle."

"Exactly!" you say, feeling validated and seen.

When your baby cries, they use their voice to alert us to their distress. We're wired to respond to their high-pitched crying. In fact, the sirens of ambulances are modeled after the cry of a baby because we have a primal need to respond to it.

Vocalizing with your baby as they cry adds an element of empathy and support that doesn't exist with just physical holding. Simply speaking in a gentle way can sometimes do the trick. But I want to offer you a way to use your voice that will calm your baby and *you*.

It starts with being aware of the *tone* of your voice. The tone of your voice is what can make you sound stressed, calm, warm, or annoyed. It communicates your feelings, temperament, and identity. Studies show that we're much more accurate at assessing the emotion of others through their voice than their face and that the tone of our voice has a huge impact on how others interpret what we say.[51],[52] Yet it's an aspect of ourselves we don't often think about.

Men tend to feel how poignantly intertwined their voice is with their identity when they go through puberty. Suddenly, songs they once sang seem too high, and people respond differently to them on the phone. Women's voices often become lower as they age or after they give birth. Joni Mitchell is a perfect example of this. When this happens, it can take a while for the identity to catch up to the new voice.

Tone of voice is so important to our identity that science has developed new ways to provide those with impaired speech with a mechanical voice that is more personalized and specific to who they are. It used to be that there were only two synthetic voices available: "Perfect Paul," which we know as Stephen Hawking's voice, and "Beautiful Betty," which we know well through Siri. But now, mechanical voices can be constructed by using the voices of family members and brain waves.

Since your baby doesn't understand your language yet, *what* you're saying is much less important. They are only listening to *how* you are saying it—to the tone of your voice and the intention behind it. Becoming more aware of your tone of voice and thinking about ways to alter it can make your soothing efforts much more effective.

HERE ARE SOME PLACES TO START USING YOUR VOICE TO SOOTHE YOUR BABY

"Who Cares?" Go with me on this. You are a parent now. You've already been through experiences with your baby that have been painful, surprising, euphoric, and humbling. You are not the person you were before having a baby. Although you may not fully feel like a grown-up—I'm not sure we ever do—you've gained a maturity that can only come from being a parent. And with it comes a deep sense of I don't give a S#&T what other people say or think. We just know too much now. And we've seen ourselves at our lowest and most glorious moments.

So who cares who is listening when you sing? Except for one person I know you care the most about. They care a whole lot.

Deep Breath In. Here's a fact: When your baby is distressed, your body goes into a state of high alert. No doubt you've experienced how stressful it can be to hear your baby crying, especially when their vocal cords are right by your ear as you try to soothe them. As you can imagine, that doesn't bode well for your voice to sound soothing.

Here's another fact: When you sing without taking in a deep breath before and between phrases, your voice will feel constricted. It may shake a bit or veer off pitch, and that will cause physical discomfort. All of this leads to a feeling of anxiety.

If you want your voice to be calming for your baby, you need to calm your body in the process. To do this you need to take in deep breaths. You'll know you are using your breath correctly when singing out almost feels like breathing out—comfortable and like a release.

Travel in Your Body. Try this exercise for a minute. Say your baby's name out loud a few times. The first time you say it, focus on your eyes. The second time you say it, focus on your belly, and the third time you say it, focus on your mouth. Did you notice a difference in the three?

Your voice can change vastly just by focusing on different areas in your body as you speak. When you focused on your eyes, perhaps your voice came out a bit higher in pitch and maybe softer in tone. When you focused on your belly, you might have used the muscles in your diaphragm, which gave you more support and made your voice louder and maybe even lower in tone. And when you moved your focus to your mouth, you might have enunciated more clearly, which made your voice sound more present, as if it was coming out of the front part of your mouth.

We sometimes experiment with this in our classes so that parents can experience how their tone and energy change just by shifting attention to different places in their body. I use this technique a lot when I record music. If I'm feeling like my voice is coming out thin, I imagine that my mouth is literally on my belly. It helps me sing from a deeper place, and my tone becomes more full.

The Voice You Wish You Had. The next time you're soothing your baby and want to sound more calm, conjure up a voice you *wish* you had. Is there someone whose voice you admire and feel is soothing? Imagine you had their voice. In fact, you can imagine you are actually them and they're soothing your baby. Let your entire tone, cadence, and melody change to sound like that person.

I do this a lot, too, when I am singing at the mic. I imagine I am someone else who I think would sound perfect singing my song—Sara Bareilles, Sam Cooke, Ed Sheeran—and I try to sing like they would. Of course, I don't sound anything like them. I still completely sound like me. But I tend to take deeper breaths and relax my body as I imagine they feel when they sing. Also, it often gets me out of overthinking and into a calmer place.

Someone Singing to You Both. This is a strange one, but stay with me on this. It works for many parents in my classes. As you are singing, try to imagine your voice is coming from *outside* you. Imagine that your voice belongs to someone else—someone who is singing to you and your baby. The idea here is that we are a lot less judgmental of others than we are of ourselves. If you can hear your voice as if it is someone else's, you'll get out of your own judgment, and you may even feel soothed by your own voice as your baby does.

Start with Small Gigs. Nobody else is invited to your rock show besides your baby. Remember, singing makes us feel vulnerable. If you don't want to sing in front of others, that's OK. Your audience of one whom you hold in your arms is enough. Other places to experiment with your voice include the shower and your car.

Practice with the Experts. Like anything, singing is about practicing and doing it a lot until it feels like second nature. Most of the time, those who don't feel comfortable singing as adults did not sing much as kids. Singing may not have been a big part of your family behavior, and maybe you just weren't exposed to it. This is one of the things you are going to change for your baby.

To make it a habit, practice with low stakes. Put on some music you love, turn it up, and sing along. Set your voice free without any inhibition. Your baby is the only one listening, and they revel in hearing you sing. So take this moment with your captive and adoring audience.

The Power of a Group. Singing in a baby class has huge benefits. I'm hoping that by the time you've done the suggestions above, you will be ready for this one. It's my favorite. It's a big reason why I do what I do. Singing in a group is *powerful*. It can feel disarming and scary but also comforting to find the right balance between being heard and hearing others.

If you join a class, I invite you to let your voice go out to the group without listening to it at all. Trust that it is going where it needs to while you focus on the other voices in the group. If you allow yourself to relax and share your voice with a group, you might feel fully present and even elated. As humans we crave connection with others. Singing together is a direct route to authentic and supportive connection.

OK, we're ready to try some vocal toning. At the end of this chapter, you'll also get a soothing method that involves rhythm, breath, and a specific, mantralike melody to sing with your baby. For now, let's just get comfortable with using your voice.

Hello Voice Exercise

(Don't just read this. Actually do it!)

Part 1:

★ Place your hand on your chest.

★ Take in a deep breath.

★ On the exhale, sigh and let your voice make a sound as you sigh.

★ Repeat a few times. Let each exhale come out with sound: it can be a high tone or a low one, or it can go from high to low.

★ Extend the sound until it's longer, holding the sound for your entire exhale.

Part 2:

★ Do the same as Part 1: Put your hand on your chest; take in a breath; and on the exhale, sing out a long note. But this time, see if you can make your sound more *resonant* (i.e., make your chest vibrate more, fill the room with your voice, make a fuller sound).

★ Try that again, exhaling and making your long tone sound full.

★ Now ask yourself: What did you need to do the second time to make your voice more resonant?

Hopefully you just tried this. As with all physical learning, we need to actually *do it* to allow for unconscious behavioral shifts to happen. When we do this exercise in class, parents often say that these were the shifts they needed to do to make their voice more resonant:

★ Take in a deeper breath.

★ Relax their jaw.

★ Use the muscles at the bottom of their belly.

★ Sing a bit louder.

★ Sit straighter.

★ Expand their lungs with the inhale.

Feeling comfortable with your voice and understanding how to use it in a more relaxed way is essential to soothing your baby and to parenting in general. Hopefully, at this point you're feeling a little more comfortable with the idea of using your voice with your baby to soothe.

Next, you'll learn a soothing method that puts all of the pieces from this section together; it soothes you at the same time as your baby, involves rhythm, and uses your voice.

Four-Step Soothing Method

1. **Bounce to the Rhythm.** In the last chapter we talked about the benefits of rhythm for your baby. Although it might sound obvious, we don't always bounce to the rhythm of a song we're singing or listening to, especially not at 3 a.m. As you're singing this mantralike melody, bounce to the rhythm of your song.

2. **Use the Vowel O.** With this method, we're not singing lyrics to a song; rather, we're simply using the o sound. This sound happens deepest in our diaphragm and as a result is lower and emulates the sound of the womb.

3. **Rock between Two Notes.** Just as you're bouncing or rocking up and down with your body, bounce with your *voice*. That means toggling between two notes, one higher and one lower. By doing this, you are bouncing your baby in an additional way besides with your arms.

4. **Take Deep Breaths between Phrases.** Your soothing techniques won't work unless your body is also relaxed. The easiest way to do that is by taking deep breaths between phrases.

Your baby changes minute by minute. Their needs change, the situation you're in shifts, and your response to your baby changes.

But you also probably know that the more tools you have in your toolbox, the better equipped you are to handle every situation. This soothing method has worked for many parents, and it might work for you. Or maybe it will work sometimes but not others. Either way, hopefully this chapter has inspired you to pay more attention to the tone of your voice and how you can use it more effectively to soothe your baby.

For a little extra encouragement, here's what a mom said after she learned this method: "During a particularly hard week of teething, my son only wanted to be held all the time. During those moments when I couldn't hold him but he was inconsolable, using the soothing song was the only thing that would calm him down. When I would have to be out of sight for a moment to get something from another room, the sound of my voice would immediately calm him, even though he wasn't being held. It is something that has continued to help us—on his first airplane trip, during school drop-off for his older sister, and in the grocery store."

There is no magic method or technique that will soothe your baby every time.

Bubble Moment: THE SOOTHING METHOD

🩶 Take in deep breaths as you soothe your baby.

🩶 Bounce to the rhythm of the song you're singing or playing.

🩶 Use the vowel sound *o* as you're vocalizing.

🩶 Toggle between two notes with your voice.

It should sound like this: *Oh, woah, woah, woah.*

Make this your own. There is no one correct way to do it.

If you'd like further inspiration, you can find a recording of this method by following this QR code:

6

It's All About You

Jana walks into class, stands by the door holding her baby, and says, "I really need this today."

During our check-ins she tells us what's going on: "Mila has been teething and waking up every hour and a half all night long. I'm so exhausted I'm not even sure I'm actually awake right now. I feel so angry at my husband because he's not helping in the middle of the night. He only takes her in the morning. I feel so angry at him. Why shouldn't I get to sleep all night?"

She starts to cry and continues: "I just feel all alone in taking care of this baby, and I can't do it all. Mila is going through a very fussy period and I keep wanting to run out of the house and cry too."

We hear you, Jana. We've *all* been there. Those weeks when it feels like too much. The lack of sleep gets to you, you're not feeling supported, and on top of all that your baby is teething, or going through a sleep regression, or is just being a baby.

I'm about to say something that might be annoying to hear: It's much easier to calm your baby when *you're* feeling calm as well. In this chapter we're going to break this down and make it doable for you so it doesn't make you want to throw this book across the room.

Show Me How to Feel

Your baby is like a little emotional antenna, constantly picking up on your subtle cues—your slight eyebrow twitch, your tapping foot, your pursed mouth—to try to understand how you feel. They're wired to make sense of the world *through* you. The way you feel is their cue for how to feel themselves.

Here's a simple illustration of how closely your baby is taking cues from your emotional state: You're in line at the grocery store, and a woman looks into the stroller and marvels at how cute your baby is. Very quickly, almost undetectably, your baby glances over at you and then back to the woman.

In that split second your baby gathers information from you—are your eyes tense? Are your lips tight? Are your eyebrows scrunched? These expressions signal to the baby that you may feel uncomfortable or view the woman as a threat. On the other hand, if they look over and see that your face is relaxed and open, they understand that the stranger is fine and they also feel calm.

Animals in the wild do the same thing. When a family of deer encounter a sound or see headlights, they freeze for a moment. The fawn quickly glances over at the parents to ascertain—are we in danger? Are we running? Are we staying?

Psychologists call this behavior in humans **social referencing**.

Social referencing is when your baby tries to understand your emotional state through your facial expression, vocal tone, and body language in order to form their own response toward other people or events in their environment. Remember body, face, voice? That's the information they're using.

Now here's the important part. When you convey to your baby that you're OK with the situation, they trust you and relax as well. The visual cliff study is a perfect demonstration of this.

In this study, babies between 9 and 12 months old are brought into the lab and put on a table with borders around it so the babies won't fall.[53] Half of the tabletop is wood and the other half is plexiglass. The plexiglass is clear and the floor can be seen underneath, so it looks like it drops, but it doesn't.

A toy is placed at the other end of the plexiglass so that the babies need to crawl over the wooden tabletop side and the plexiglass side to reach it.

The babies want to reach the toy, but when they approach the plexiglass with the visible drop, they hesitate. And then what do they do? You guessed it—they look to their mother.

They search her face to find signs—is she relaxed? Smiling? Nervous? Tense? And they keep moving forward only when they're satisfied that their mother shows no sign of stress. Her facial expression is enough to convince them that what looks very scary is actually safe.

What a huge amount of power your face, body, and voice have on your baby!

How can you use this information? The next time your baby seems fussy or uncomfortable, ask yourself what *your* emotional state is. There's a chance they are picking up on your discomfort or anxiety.

Here are a few tips for helping your baby understand the world through your own state of mind.

Own It. Simply being aware of the fact that your baby is seeking your cues may make you more careful about what you are conveying to your baby.

Tune In. I'm talking about tuning in to yourself this time. So much of parenting is focusing on your baby and being sensitive to their emotional state. But the only way to be clearer about what you are transmitting to your baby is to first become aware of how *you* feel. This is easier said than done. So often we interact with others and aren't fully aware of the fact that we don't feel comfortable with them and that tension is building up in our body. Tune in to your belly, your jaw, your eyes. Your body will give you clues to how you feel in that moment.

Be Authentic. This can be a tough one. Sometimes you might have a feeling on the inside but try to convey something else on the outside. When you feel ambivalent, your baby may be confused and have a hard time discerning how to make sense of the situation. We can't always do this, but try to sync your behavior with your expression. Here's an example: Your baby wakes you up again at night. You're feeling grumpy and resentful, but you don't want your baby to get the worst of you. You try to channel your inner Mary Poppins and say, "Hi, my love!" There is a chance you might be able to shift your mood just by taking in a breath and forcing a smile. But if you find yourself straining to act differently than you're feeling, let down the act. Your baby will know anyway. As the years go on, you want them to trust you.

Relax Your Face. Especially when your baby is doing new things, like trying new food, climbing up to the slide, or learning how to crawl or walk, they are going to look to you for reassurance. In those moments you can take a breath and try to keep your face relaxed and your expression open and positive. If you manage to impart the message that "it's OK, you got this!" in a convincing manner, they'll believe it.

It's Not Working

You've tried to calm your baby, you're trying to calm yourself, but it's not working. You're so tired, you can't take another soothing match, and you're frustrated and angry at the situation. The questions flood in—*what am I doing wrong? What does my baby need?* And at the bottom of it all: *Am I a good parent?*

That's OK, it's normal.

Remember, simply by holding your baby and trying to figure out what they need, you're already doing your job of loving them, working to attune to them, and not turning your back on their distress even when it's uncomfortable for you.

Successful soothing is not measured by whether your baby calms down but by your willingness to be there with them in their distress. Even if your baby is not immediately soothed at that moment, you're doing great.

In those moments remind yourself, *I'm OK, my baby is OK, I'm giving my baby love and support.* And then, while quieting your own mind, work to relax your body.

And how do you do that? You fake it till you make it.

Fake It Till You Make It

I can hear you now. "It's pretty hard to even pretend to feel calm when my baby is freaking out."

Yes, it is *very* stressful when your baby is crying on your shoulder and you're doing everything to calm them. Your body goes into high alert by raising your cortisol levels and your heart rate, making your body ready for action and response. If you were a chef it would feel like the cake is burning, the soup is overflowing, and you just nicked your finger cutting the vegetables.

As you react to your baby, your baby reacts to your stress levels rising, and vice versa. You've got a nice feedback loop—they get more stressed, you do as a response, they escalate in response to you, and on and on. The only way your baby will start to calm is if you do.

To fake it till you make it you need to trick your body into thinking you're calm. Use what science has taught us about how to calm our nervous system. Take deep breaths (between phrases if you're vocalizing), bounce to the rhythm, relax your belly, and drop your shoulders. If you can focus on making small adjustments in your body, even while your baby is screaming in your ear and you're not feeling relaxed *at all*, it will end up working.

Soothing Methods That Work

There are many soothing methods out there. You've probably already found videos claiming that *this* is the ultimate soothing method, which might be the case. But most likely, you'll have a bunch that work at different times.

But there will be one common element to the ones that work: They'll soothe *you* as they soothe the baby. This is an often-overlooked point. Most techniques are missing this crucial element. The strategies are so focused on calming the baby but disregard the one who's holding the baby.

For your soothing method to work, it must soothe *you* too.

How can you know if your soothing method soothes you while calming your baby?

The next time you're soothing your baby, check if the way you soothe:

○ Regulates your breath
○ Relaxes your body
○ Incorporates rhythm in a consistent way

The soothing method offered in Chapter 5 works for many parents because it uses voice in a way that massages you inside your body, regulates your breathing, and keeps you in sync with your baby. By singing the sound *o*, making a resonant sound, taking deep breaths in between sounds, and singing on a regular rhythm, you're making your breaths in and out more even. This is very similar to a mantra. Mantras have been shown to be effective because they quiet the mind, regulate the breath, and provide a repetitive rhythmic focus.[54]

But it might not work for you, and that's OK. Find the method that feels calming for you first and foremost.

Don't Forget Your Voice

Your voice can convey tension when you don't even realize it. When we are stressed, our voice tends to crack more, it is usually higher in tone, and we feel out of breath when we speak.

Fake It Till You Make It with Voice:

1. **Take in deep breaths between phrases.** This allows for your vocalizations to feel more supported and full. Otherwise you'll run out of breath and end up tensing your body even more to get the sound out.

2. **Lower your tone.** Imagine you're a celebrity who has a low voice you find soothing. Emulate their voice. Imagining we have someone else's voice is a great way to get out of our head and find a more resonant side of our voice.

3. **Speak or sing slower.** Emulate a preschool teacher with this one. She speaks slower because it calms the kids, but it also keeps her from spinning out when the blocks are flying, four kids need to pee, and it's time for lunch.

Extra Tips for Relaxing Your Face:

* Pick up the corners of your mouth ever so slightly.
* Massage your forehead, moving to your temples.
* Massage your jaw. (We hold so much tension there!)
* Massage behind your ears.

Post-Baby System Alert

After I had my daughter, I went through a phase in which I was so on edge. I would see something in the corner of my eye, like a piece of fuzz or a shadow, and I'd jump out of my seat with my heart beating like a drum.

Turns out, it was normal. It was my primal brain geared up to fiercely protect my baby. It's the same instinct a bird has as she sits on her nest, watching for threats, or an octopus as she feeds her offspring.

These days there are usually no animals threatening to attack our baby, and there's less of a need for us to be on guard. But with everything happening right now in your life, your protective stress hormones might be vibrating with a heightened fight or flight response.

Pair that with lack of sleep, isolation, and boredom, and you've got a perfect storm. You picked up this book because you wanted to learn how to be a better parent to your baby. It starts with *being a compassionate parent to yourself.*

Since we're grown-ups now, it's based on the honor code: You grade yourself. This means *you* decide if you've reached your threshold and need outside help, or if you can find ways to give yourself what you need and maintain your physical and mental health.

Mental/Physical Health Inventory

HOW MANY HOURS OF SLEEP ARE YOU GETTING?

This is a huge topic, I know. You're probably hoping your baby will start sleeping through the night *really* soon. You think, *maybe they will once they stop teething, coughing, feeding at night, or forget the old pacifier.*

While you can't fully control your baby's sleep patterns, you can take care of yours. You know this, but it's worth saying here again because it's so important:

○ Go to sleep early so that you get some deep sleep before possible wake-ups.

○ Don't automatically start the next episode of the show you're watching. That takes Herculean effort, I know.

○ Try to make your bed a non-screen zone, or at least put your phone in the other room when you can.

HOW ALIGNED (NOT TONED) DOES YOUR BODY FEEL?

You probably don't have too much time to go to the gym right now, so I'm not even going to suggest it. But here are two tips that will make all the difference:

○ **Commit to five minutes of stretching a day.** Holding a baby is a ton of physical work. It is a huge strain on your body. Stretching for five minutes a day will help you feel so much better and will help you sleep better.

○ **Try to stand up straight.** Put your bag on the other shoulder every now and then; bring your chin back slightly so that your neck is long and lift your chest. You don't want to end your baby's first year straightening like a crumpled paper being flattened out.

HOW KIND ARE YOU BEING TO YOURSELF?

If you're like me when I had little babies, you are having extreme highs and lows, often in the same hour. So, first of all, know that this will not last forever. This is not your new state as a parent. You *will* feel more emotionally stable as time goes on.

Be kind to yourself during this time. During any time really. You're working hard to tune in to your baby. Now see if you can turn that same level of compassion and patience toward yourself. To them you may be saying a version of "I love you. I'm listening." Today, try saying that to yourself.

You need as much soothing as your baby does. Be compassionate not just to your baby but to yourself.

Take a moment. Take some deep breaths. And say to yourself, *I love you and I am listening.* Now see what comes up.

FOCUS ON THE MICRO

When we feel overwhelmed by things beyond our reach and control, the best remedy is to focus on what *is* OK, what *is* going right, and what we *do* have. Ask yourself, *in this very moment, am I OK? Is my baby OK?* Most likely the answer is yes. Now be *here.* Focus on how it feels to touch your baby, notice their smell, their sounds, and even their taste. Narrow your vision to what is right in front of you, and through that you'll expand your vision and experience.

WHEN WAS THE LAST TIME YOU ASKED FOR HELP?

During this very challenging year with your baby, ask for what you need.

Maybe it's a break from waking up with the baby at night. Tell your partner or get a night nurse. Maybe you need a couple days away so you can sleep well and feel yourself again. Ask a family member, partner, or sitter to watch your baby during that time. Maybe you need to feel less alone in all of this. Ask your friends to check in more often, even if you can't always answer.

Here's what Alexa said in class: "My friend isn't a mom and I miss her so much. The thing is, she always calls during the witching hour, right when I'm in the thick of parenting. I don't want to miss out on her calls and I don't want her to feel like everything changed, but I just can't answer at that time. But everything did change for me, and I guess she needs to know that. I need her to know that I need her and need her to keep calling but that we'll have to figure out a different time to talk."

People are usually grateful when we tell them what we need. Most likely, if Alexa told her friend they needed to find a different time to chat, they'd be happy to oblige. She's probably been getting frustrated by the fact that Alexa is distracted when they speak. Give those around you an opportunity to have a mini superhero moment and help you. Let them know where they can swoop in and save the day.

Digging Deeper

Now let's peel back the layers. How you feel doesn't just affect your ability to soothe. It has a huge impact on your connection with your baby and thus, of course, their well-being.

Attachment theory teaches us that your ability to develop a secure bond with your baby depends on **your inner state**—your emotions, your relationships with those around you, your childhood experiences, and your mental health.

In the last section we talked about tending to your acute physical needs, but to truly be present with your baby, see them for who they are, and respond effectively to their needs, you have to become more aware of deeper emotions and often unconscious harmful patterns.

Caring for a baby can bring up feelings that have been buried since we were babies ourselves. When I had my first baby, I remember thinking a lot about how it felt for my mother and father to

hold me, how they felt as new parents, how
they looked at me in their arms. I was flooded
with memories from my childhood and saw them
through a different prism, with a little more compassion sprinkled into the anger.

But here's the thing. The feelings being a parent
brings up for you, including those induced by hormones,
lack of sleep, and identity shift, have *nothing* to do with what's going
on for your baby and everything to do with *your* own experience.
And those are just the ones you're aware of.

All of us learned how to try to get the love and attachment we
needed as kids. But some of those behaviors, while survival mech-
anisms, are harmful to us today. For instance, we learned how to
take care of others, hide our emotions, retreat into solitude, or
lash out as ways to cope when we weren't getting the connection we
needed. But now those patterns aren't serving us as well and may
even be damaging to our babies (and thrust them into unhealthy
patterns of their own).

To see your baby "as is," without your lens being clouded by your
own past experience, you need to become more aware of how your
patterns of behavior look when they arise, and why you cultivated
them in the first place. Otherwise, you risk playing out those same
dynamics with your baby and the cycle continues.

It takes being honest with yourself and, even better, with a professional therapist who can help you undo years and even generations of repeated emotional harm.

But here's the good news. If you are able to confront your difficult childhood experiences head-on, that same pain can actually
turn into power.

Your Parenting Superpower

I remember one day when I was at therapy, talking about why I feel so strongly about helping parents *see* their baby and connect to them.

She said, "That's what you wanted to get as a baby but didn't."

The tears that immediately welled up in my eyes made me realize she was right.

So much of what I teach and what I work hard to give my kids (but don't always succeed) is what I needed desperately as a baby but didn't always get.

We all have childhood trauma on some level. It's inevitable. Your baby will, too, no matter how mindful you are with your parenting. Harmful behaviors are passed down through generations and are sometimes so ingrained in us that any other behavior seems odd.

What was most traumatic for you might just turn into your parenting superpower.

These patterns can become obstacles that we can't seem to overcome no matter how hard we try, like the friend we keep around despite feeling hurt every time we see them. Home feels like home—familiar and comfortable—no matter how harmful it is.

But every now and then, when we put in the work to understand our traumas and what left us feeling abandoned, neglected, or distressed as children, we're able to make magic happen.

What was most traumatic for you might just turn into your parenting superpower.

If you can take the time to figure it out, you may be able to push against it, soften, and turn to the world with a burning desire to correct your experience. The world will benefit from your scar, and your child will feel your passion to make sure they don't have the same issue.

They may have others, but not that one.

Your biggest job, besides keeping your baby safe, is to mind your inner state so that you can turn your traumas around, convert them into love for your baby, and then, dear parent, get out of their way and let them be who they are.

• •

Recap: TIPS FOR SOOTHING YOUR BABY:

1. **Use a soothing method that soothes you** at the same time as it soothes your baby.
2. **Fake it till you make it— take deep breaths,** calm your body, relax your face, lower your voice, slow your movements.
3. **Take a break and walk away** for a minute if you need to.
4. **Tune in to what *you* need at that moment to know what your baby needs.** Maybe it's a walk outside. Maybe it's a song.
5. **Tune in to what your baby's distress is bringing up for you.** Put a pin in it and process it with a therapist or friend.

• •

The other day one of the moms in class shared a difficult moment she had and how she tuned in to what she needed to get through it. She said:

"I was trying to put my baby to sleep and it was after a day of him barely napping. I was at it for more than an hour, and he just wouldn't go to sleep. He was overtired and fussy. I wanted to cry. I felt myself getting so angry at him. Once I realized that, I put him down in his crib and walked out of the room. He was crying, but I got a glass of water, sat for a minute, and then got down on the floor and did a child's pose. After a few minutes, I went back in a little more collected and was able to put him to sleep."

This mama was working so hard to soothe her baby and was

slowly getting worked up herself. Eventually she realized that she herself needed to be held and soothed. She found a way to do that getting into a fetal position on the floor and taking in deep breaths.

Bubble Moment: BABY CALM MOMENT

💜 As you pick up your baby, notice where in your body you feel stressed.

💜 Imagine that area filling with breath as you inhale. Imagine it melting as you exhale.

💜 Take in deep breaths through your nose and exhale through your mouth.

💜 Maybe use a mantra like "I'm OK, my baby is OK, we're OK together," or "I can handle this. I love and support my baby. This will pass."

PART 3

. . . .

THE
PERFECT
PASTIMES

7

Relax and Enjoy
the Show

THIS CHAPTER IS ABOUT HOW TO PLAY WITH
YOUR BABY IN A WAY THAT IS RELAXING FOR
YOU AND BOOSTS THEIR INDEPENDENCE
AND CURIOSITY.

Class just ended and parents are packing up. A dad asks if I can watch his baby while he uses the restroom, and I gladly oblige. I love these stolen moments. I sit down next to the baby, and she glances over at me. There's a moment of recognition in her gaze. At this point she's familiar with me and turns her attention back to her toy. Suddenly, she sees a ball of fuzz on the carpet and tries to grab it. She looks at her hand, wondering if she's holding it, but then looks back and realizes it's still on the carpet. She tries again. Once the fuzz is in her hand, she tries to squeeze it but seems surprised that there's not much to hold on to. We're both transfixed by the fuzz. Dad walks into the room and says, "What are you both looking at?"

In the next couple of chapters we're talking about *play*: how important it is for your baby's social and cognitive development, how it can turn a meltdown into merriment, and how to do it with as little effort as possible.

This chapter's approach is one of my favorites to lead in class.

It's when we expand parents' perception of play from purely interactive, which can feel demanding and exhausting, and focus on a type of play that parents don't often consider but is just as important. Maybe you identify with Johann: "I always feel like I need to entertain my baby or like I should be teaching him something. I sit at home thinking, *Should I be reading a book to him right now? Singing the ABCs? Is that what all the other dads are doing? It seems like it. But I'm way too tired for that.*"

We really do drive ourselves crazy, right? It's an epidemic of this generation. Even though parents these days spend a lot more time with their babies compared to parents before the '90s, we fear we're not spending enough time, doing enough, enriching enough.[55]

We plow through articles warning us that not doing the right thing now may have an impact on when a baby starts speaking, which will impact how well they do in school, which college they get into, and how affluent they'll be as adults.[56] Ack! That's a lot riding on *Brown Bear, Brown Bear, What Do You See?*

We see other babies rolling, crawling, standing, or talking earlier than our baby, and we feel a competitive itch. We take on the challenge to "enrich" our baby like a project we're determined to ace. The problem is we don't always stop to consider exactly what that means. In this era of involved parenting, we understand it as being *active*, teaching, showing, somehow infusing our baby with knowledge.

I know this all firsthand. I was the alpha mom fueled by stress who went into overdrive to make sure I was doing it "right."

It wasn't until I had my third baby that I learned the most important lesson.

Our Babies Actually Don't Need Us to Do What *We* Think We Need to Do

They don't need us to actively show them things, instruct, or demonstrate. They're born scientists, constantly investigating their surroundings. They're looking for patterns, taking note of repetitions and anomalies, and watching us very closely. We think we're the PhDs and our babies are the students. But they just need us to be their lab assistants.

This chapter is all about how to encourage your baby's exploration so they'll feel safe and inspired to follow their curiosity without you needing to do much. If you do it right, eventually your baby won't need you there at all. But for now your presence can play a big part in their research.

Magda Gerber

In 1939 a woman named Magda Gerber took her daughter to see a pediatrician in Budapest named Emmi Pikler. Their meeting changed the landscape of early care forever.

Gerber was taken with the way Emmi Pikler communicated with her child. It was different from the other pediatricians she had gone to. Pikler seemed to have more respect for the child. Gerber noticed that her daughter, and all of Pikler's patients, responded to the doctor with their full cooperation.

> "Be careful what you teach. It might interfere with what they are learning." —Magda Gerber

Inspired, Gerber pursued a degree in early childhood education and went to work with Pikler. In 1957, Gerber immigrated with her family to the United States and founded the Pilot Infant Program at the Dubnoff School, taking what she'd learned from Pikler and developing a novel approach to baby care.

R-E-S-P-E-C-T . . . Find Out
What It Means to Me

Gerber's program was founded on the belief that caregivers must honor an infant's fundamental right to autonomy despite their extreme dependence on adults. She believed that balancing both truths, the utter dependence with the desire for independence, laid the foundation for lifelong resilience and a relationship based on mutual respect.[57]

Especially in the first months, it can be hard to see your baby as a person and not just an eating/sleeping/pooping machine. But with time, we learn that honoring an infant's autonomy means acknowledging their "otherness"—that their desires and pace are different from our own.

How would this look in day-to-day interactions, according to Gerber? Before changing your baby's diaper, you'd invite them to participate by explaining what's about to happen. Instead of just seeing them as a passive participant, you'd allow your baby a moment to absorb the communication through your voice, gestures, and eyes, and understand what's expected of them. In this way you're viewing them as a partner in the task even though they need you to do the handiwork.

When we rush into action without conferring with our baby, we miss out on developing cooperation and, even more importantly, connection. Hammond illustrates Gerber's approach well in her article about Gerber's work:

"If she [the parent] believes that the baby is capable of participating in the activity, and invites him to cooperate, the care will proceed slowly and be rich with reciprocal communication as they work together to be understood. If, however, the adult thinks of the baby as oblivious and incapable of cooperation, expecting him to be passive and compliant, the task may be quickly accomplished but the joy of togetherness will be missing."[58]

This may seem familiar and obvious, because Gerber's ideas (and those of other contributors, such as Bowlby, Stern, Trevarthon, and Brazelton) have become so prevalent in caregiving today. But Gerber's approach was revolutionary at the time and even now can lead us to a new way of thinking about *play*.

The Mode in Between

Imagine a spectrum of modes of being with your baby:

ON ONE SIDE: INTERACTIVE, PARENT LED

You're sitting with your baby—playing, singing "The Itsy Bitsy Spider" and doing the hand motions, or are reading them a book, giving them a bath, or playing with them with a toy. This mode is *interactive*. *You're leading the play*, and you're both engaged with each other and share a point of attention.

ON THE OTHER SIDE: NON-INTERACTIVE, BABY LED

Your baby is happily playing with a toy on the carpet. You're nearby in the kitchen with one eye on the baby and the other on the dishes. This mode is *non-interactive*. In this mode your baby is content and occupying themselves while you're doing something else. In this mode your *baby is leading the play*. They're deciding what to do and how.

We tend to think of these as the only two modes of being with babies. But there's another in the middle of the spectrum, and it's equally important, if not more. How would it look if *your baby led the play and you were both fully engaged*?

IN THE MIDDLE MODE: ENGAGED, BABY LED

Your baby leads the play and you follow along. You don't have face-to-face engagement, but you have a shared focal point. You aren't completely passive or disengaged; rather, you are active in your observing. You are completely present and are mindful of your baby's experience. I call this mode the **Explorer State**.

The Explorer State

Imagine a parent sitting on the floor with their baby and a friend. They're watching their baby while having a conversation with their friend. Their observation of their baby is somewhat absent-minded. They're on the ready if the baby needs them, but they aren't fully present with the baby.

That's a perfect mode of parenting and one you probably inhabit often—you're close enough to the baby to take care of them and keep them out of danger, but you're also satisfying your own needs for connection, getting stuff done, or overcoming boredom. Great! But that's not what we're aiming for in this chapter.

In the Explorer State, you'll not just observe your baby in their play but you'll join their perspective. You'll attempt to *feel* their experience with them. Through this process you learn what makes your baby tick.

Your baby is in an Explorer State all day. The challenge of this activity is for *you* to join them in this state. We can't do this all day. Most of the time you're busy doing baby care tasks. During those moments, like with diaper changing, you can observe and interact mindfully.

But for a few moments a day you can take your observation further by joining them in their Explorer State.

Learning how to see the world through your baby's perspective takes practice. In fact, having empathy for anyone's perspective other than our own takes years of practice and therapy to understand where our own vision gets snagged on past traumas.

Here's what I say in class to help parents join their baby in exploration: "Get into a position where your head is next to your baby's head. If your baby is lying on their back, lie down next to them.

If they're on their belly, lie on your belly next to them. If they're sitting, lie on your belly in a way that your head is at their head's height.

"Notice where your baby's attention is. Are they looking at a toy they're holding or that you're holding? Are they looking at something farther away, like a tree out the window or something on the ceiling? What seems interesting to them?"

It usually takes the parents a minute to settle into the exercise. At first they instinctively do what they normally do—stare at their beautiful and fascinating baby. It's what we spend so much of our time doing. How can we not?

But this exercise calls for something different. The goal is to look at your baby not to admire them but to find out *where they're looking* or what they're hearing, touching, smelling, tasting. And then it's to imagine what those experiences *feel* like.

Why is your baby turning the toy around and putting one particular part in their mouth? Perhaps that part feels different on their tongue. Imagine how it feels. Is your baby nuzzling up against your arm? Perhaps they're smelling it. Are they touching the rug? How might it feel for them?

"The first thing I realized was how many hours my baby spends staring at the ceiling! I never thought about it. It's so boring! But then I noticed she was looking at the ceiling fan. She stared at it forever, just looking at the shapes. I looked with her and it was pretty interesting." (Joanna, mom of Rishi)

Great! Now I Can Get Stuff Done!

"I do this all the time! The other day I was in the kitchen straightening up and my baby was lying on the floor playing for like an hour." (Marsha, mom of Connor)

I get this comment every now and then. Marsha, that's some well-deserved *you* time that you absolutely need during your day. But it's not the Explorer State. Gerber talked about *observation* without judgment or agenda. But observation can also be construed as *passive* or even not fully present. To be in the Explorer State and reap the benefits for yourself and your baby, your observation needs to be *passively active*.

In this instance, you might not be physically active, which might look passive to someone watching, but you're mindfully active. Your attention is alert. It's not as energy demanding as the interactive mode, but it does take focus and mind control.

Think of it like meditating or, better yet, like taking a meditative walk or swim. Your task, for that period of time, is to try to stay focused on your senses—how the ground feels beneath your feet, how the breeze feels on your cheek, the nature sounds around you. Buddhist meditation often starts with focusing on our senses because it's what's happening in this moment. It's the most reliable way to be present, to have our attention on what we are experiencing *right now*, as opposed to getting lost in thoughts.

Similarly, in the Explorer State, you're observing your baby and imagining what they might be sensing. Your own senses need to be awake and alert to do so. Every time your attention wanders, which it will, your job is to bring it back by glancing at your baby to see what they're interested in.

Three Reasons It Is Important for You to Be *Mentally* Present and Not Just Physically Present

1. **Because your baby will notice**

   Try this experiment at home—First, do the Explorer State when you are physically and mentally present, sharing a focal point with your baby.

   Next, lie next to them while holding your phone. You probably already know exactly what happens. Within a few seconds your baby will notice that you're not with them and start to complain.

Your baby has a Jedi sense for when you're not present with them, even if you're looking straight at them. They sense when your attention is elsewhere.

If you want your baby to learn how to play for longer and eventually explore fully on their own, support them with your attention now. Not all the time, just a few moments a day.

2. **Because it's calming for *you***

"We did the Explorer State this week and I couldn't believe how *relaxing* it was! Until now I've been driving myself crazy thinking I needed to entertain her all the time and keep her occupied. She was so happy playing next to me and played longer than she ever has! And I got to just lie next to her and watch what she did." (Brianna, mom of Caleb)

Getting into the Explorer State with your baby lets *you* chill out. You get to actually relax for a minute, knowing that what you're doing is enriching your baby and helping them develop their curiosity, dexterity, and creativity. No need for the song and dance.

3. **Because it may elicit a feeling of *awe***

You might be thinking, *I watch my baby all the time. I know their every move. No mystery there!* But sometimes we see the broad strokes and forget to focus on the details. Surprising revelations occur when we observe something we know so well with curiosity and wonder.

I remember sitting with my baby daughter outside one day. I was feeling so exhausted, so I put down a blanket and laid next to her as she sat, looking around. At some point she picked up a dried leaf and crinkled it in her hands. She was fascinated by the feel of it, the sound it made, how it crumbled into small pieces, how those pieces fell to the ground. And because I was present to her awe, I was right there with her. I was in awe of a dried leaf that normally I would have disregarded.

Why is it good to be in awe? Because it increases our positive mood and feeling of connectedness, and it decreases materialism.[59]

The Explorer State in Action

BIRTH TO 3 MONTHS

○ Your baby is lying on their back and you are lying next to them, holding up a toy. You aren't manipulating it; rather, you are letting your baby simply look at it.

○ Your baby is on their tummy and you pull up the middle of a burp cloth to create a tent in front of them. Your baby is examining the cloth and you are looking with them. You're noticing what their eyes are drawn to—maybe not even to the toy or cloth at all.

○ You're lying next to them and looking at them to see where they're looking. Where is their gaze? What's holding their interest? Are they trying to grab something?

4 TO 8 MONTHS

○ Your baby is lying down or sitting while holding a toy, paci, or burp cloth on their own and turning it around, putting it in their mouth.

○ You're lying down next to them on your back if they are on their back, or on your belly if they're sitting.

○ You're noticing how they're moving the toy around. What colors are they interested in? What shapes? Which textures do they want to put in their mouth to explore the object further? Often babies put the same part of a toy in their mouth over and over. Do you notice that they have such a preference? Perhaps they aren't looking at the toy at all but, rather, outside or across the room. What are they focusing on? What do they hear? Smell?

9 TO 12 MONTHS

○ Your baby is on the move, either crawling or walking. They're finding things on their way that interest them—picking up toys, examining them, and then continuing on.

○ You're following your baby at their level, either sitting next to them or crouching.

○ You're noticing what draws your baby's attention. What are they drawn to and want to touch and explore? Do they pull anything into their mouth to explore it further? What is it? What types of things interest your baby? Now that they're on the move, they have much more control over what they can touch and explore.

○ Tip for this age: Have a *yes* space where everything is fair play and they can't get into too much trouble (outlets, sharp objects, etc.)

Resisting the Urge to Lead

For some parents, it's hard to do more. For others, it's hard to do *less*. When we do this activity in class, I notice that some parents find it difficult to simply hold a toy above their baby. Instead they wave it around to catch the baby's attention, or with an older baby they show the "correct" way to play with a toy.

Here's the thing—you want your baby to grow into a self-learner. You want them to be that kid whose interest is sparked by something they see and they go investigate it on their own. You know what will help develop your little researcher? Letting your baby figure it out on their own.

Researcher and child psychiatrist Stuart Brown, who founded the National Institute for Play, writes in his book *Play: How It Shapes the Brain, Opens Imagination, and Invigorates the Soul*: "All evidence indicates that the greatest rewards of play come when it arises naturally from within. When play arises out of innate motivations it is also likely timed to occur when we are primed for the most synaptic neural growth."[60]

Knowing When to Intervene

There's a beautiful scene in a video by Magda Gerber called On Their Own *with Our Help*.[61] In the video a few babies are happily playing. One of them crawls under a low table to explore and finds himself stuck, not knowing how to get out. At some point he becomes distressed and cries.

Gerber goes over to the baby and lies down near him. She empathizes with his crying by vocally mirroring his cries. She puts her hand over his head to make sure he's not knocking it and hurting himself. But she doesn't move the table or pull him out. She patiently waits for the baby to find his way out from under the table. I say *patiently* because for me those few seconds while the baby cried were excruciating but inspiring. Eventually, the baby crawls out and Gerber takes him into her arms and hugs him until he calms down.

Knowing when to intervene and when to let your baby work through frustration is not easy. On the one hand you want to be hands-off, respect your baby's autonomy, and encourage their problem-solving skills. On the other hand, you want to help your baby if they are feeling distress and give them the confidence that you are there, supporting them when they need you.

This comes back to the *pause* from Chapter 3. Unless your baby is truly hurt or in danger, the only way to know if they can tolerate their discomfort is to give it a moment. It's tempting to instinctively show your baby how to put the square block into the square hole when they're frustrated. If your baby reaches a high level of distress, you may very well need to do that. But as a rule of thumb, it's always a good idea to be there, empathize, perhaps gently assist, but not do it for the baby unless needed.

How It Feels to Be a Baby

The Explorer State is about embodying your baby's experience, matching their attention, and attempting to sense what they sense. But it's hard to truly understand your baby's point of view. Luckily, researcher Alison Gopnik's work helps.

She says that babies are very good at taking in lots of information from different sources at once. It's hard for us to imagine. As adults, we've learned to *focus* on one thing at a time. We've also become accustomed to the world around us. It takes a lot to surprise us. But your baby is in a state of constantly taking in *all* of the newness around them. They're flooded with neurotransmitters that induce learning and plasticity, but the inhibitory parts of their brain haven't been activated yet. "When people say that babies can't pay attention, it's more that they're bad at paying attention to one thing," Gopnik says.

Adults can't survive in that realm all the time. We need to get stuff done! And that takes planning, narrowing down our focus, and a lot of executive function. But your baby isn't concerned with planning for the future. They're concerned with figuring out how the world in front of them works. You can actually see them weighing objects, feeling shapes, assessing temperatures, experimenting with gravity, and identifying patterns. This means that in order to get into the Explorer State with your baby, you might need to put some effort into opening your senses to everything around you and being willing to be guided by your and your baby's *experience* rather than your thoughts.

. . . .

Recap: WHY THE EXPLORER STATE IS SO GOOD FOR YOU *AND* YOUR BABY

1. **It's Relaxing.** This activity is good for your baby, but more than anything it's good for *you*. It gives you a minute to be present with your baby while not being active. It's like a meditation break.

2. **It's a Mood Booster.** While joining your baby in their play you might just find yourself in awe, which will reconnect you to the beauty in the world and pull you out of one-more-bottle-to-wash mode.

3. **It's Enriching for Your Baby.** All you have to do is lie down next to them and watch them play for a few minutes, and it helps your baby's mental and physical development. No flash cards necessary!

4. **It Can Increase Your Baby's Focus.** Your baby will be able to play autonomously knowing you are there with them, which will increase their ability to play independently when you are farther away.

5. **You Learn Who Your Baby Is.** By closely observing your baby, you learn which objects interest them, which senses they are most led by, when they get frustrated, and when to let them work it out on their own.

. . . .

Bubble Moment: EXPLORER STATE

💜 Pick the right time. Find a moment when your baby is content, not hungry or tired.

💜 Join your baby in the same position they are in. If they're lying down, lie down next to them. If they're sitting and playing, sit next to them. If they are on the move, walk with them and explore what they're exploring.

💜 Be curious. Your main question is: How does the world look and feel for my baby? The answer lies in you asking many questions: What is my baby looking at? Are they holding something? Are they moving around? What is their path? Are they gazing out the window? At what? Are they looking at me? Are they exploring a toy?

💜 Try to experience what they are experiencing. Try to imagine what they're feeling in their hands or in their mouth.

💜 You don't need to say or do anything. Your baby is doing it all for themself. You are just there to be present with them in their exploration and get a lesson from them on how to be present in play.

💜 Look at your baby solely to see where they are looking.

💜 Let them teach you how to truly examine something that you may have taken for granted for years.

8

The Only Game
You Need

IN THIS CHAPTER YOU'LL LEARN HOW TO
DEVELOP YOUR LANGUAGE OF PLAY WITH
YOUR BABY AND ADD LAUGHTER AND
LEARNING TO YOUR DAY.

It's a breezy spring day, and Ashleigh, one of the moms in our class, arrives early. She pulls her baby out of the stroller, holds him with one hand, and does the impossible parenting balancing act of holding everything else in her other hand. Her baby watches her like an audience with popcorn at the circus.

As Ashleigh pulls the blanket out of the bag, she loses her grip on the bottle and it falls. She's frustrated and is about to bend down and get it when she notices her baby giggling. Suddenly, she sees the humor in all of it too. She picks up the bottle, holds it for a minute, looks at her baby, and drops it again to see if it elicits the same response. Her baby giggles louder now, and so does mom. Mom picks up the bottle with some Charlie Chaplin flair this time, exaggerating the effort it takes to bend down with the baby in her arms. She holds it for a second and looks at her baby with an "anticipation face"—eyebrows high and a slight smile—before dropping it again. Parents start to arrive at the door and the duo's attention shifts.

Have you had a version of this happen? If not, you will. Once your baby starts laughing, you'll do anything to hear it again. Then back-and-forths like this one will happen daily, even for a short Bubble Moment right before class.

In the last chapter we talked about your baby leading play and you going along for an enlightening and relaxing ride. This chapter focuses on interactive play and explains how there's really just one type of game that you'll be playing with millions of variations.

Play is a prolonged and positive synchronized interaction with your baby.

"I felt kind of bored with my baby. I mean, I loved when I looked at her and she laughed and I laughed too. And sometimes I sing to her or we go for a walk. But after trying what we learned in our last class I feel like I can actually play with my baby! It's so much more fun." (Nicole, mom of Amari)

So let's get to it!

What Is Interactive *Play*?

You have endless interactions with your baby every day. Which ones would you define as "play"? Are they moments in which your baby isn't crying? Or in which you're interacting with each other? Or in which you're both smiling?

If you stop to consider what you would classify as play with your baby, you may notice that these moments have a few common characteristics:

- **They're Absorbing.** You and your baby are interested in what you're doing, no matter how brief.
- **They Are for Their Own Sake.** You're not trying to achieve a particular outcome or response.
- **They Feel More Special.** These moments are a departure from rote tasks and normal living.

Your baby (and you) can engage in play with another person and also on their own. In this chapter we'll focus on *interactive* play.

How Do You Go from *Humdrum* to *Fun*?

In 1955 Dutch anthropologist Johan Huizinga set out to define play in his book *Homo Ludens*. He said, "Play is a free activity standing quite consciously outside 'ordinary' life as being 'not serious,' but at the same time absorbing the player intensely and utterly."

But how do you step out of ordinary life? Most of life, and certainly life with a baby, consists of rote tasks that feel habitual after a while. Heating a bottle, wiping a stinky butt, or trying to soothe a fussy baby can feel like the opposite of play.

Well, in large part, it's up to you. But don't worry. You don't need to go out and get a clown costume. For an activity to be outside the ordinary, it doesn't need to be a novel activity. It just needs to *feel* different. And that comes down to how you view the 1,056th time you change the baby's diaper or fold a sock.

Daily Synchrony

During your daily interactions, you and your baby engage in what psychologists call "parent-infant synchrony."[62] It occurs when you match each other's behavior, affect, and biological rhythms, often without even realizing it.

Beatrice Beebe is a researcher who has been investigating the communication between parents and babies since the 1970s. Continuing the work of Daniel Stern, she set out to closely observe interactions between parents and babies through video microanalysis. By slowing down videos that showed the parent's face and the baby's face as they interacted, she was able to analyze responses they had to each other. She noticed something fascinating.

In these microsecond analyses, she found that parents and babies instinctually react to each other's slightest movements, facial expressions, and vocalizations. Not only that, they're often *coordinated*, much like a dance.

For instance, the baby furrows their brow slightly, and a microsecond later or sometimes even concurrently, the mother does as well. The mother raises her arm to touch the baby, and even before it lands on her baby's head, the baby moves their leg or arm in coordination with her movement.

It's probably not surprising that Beebe found that high levels of synchrony predicted secure attachment years later. It makes sense—the parent who naturally coordinates movements with their baby is probably more attentive to them. Meanwhile, the baby is doing the same—learning how to attune themself to the parent.

Beebe and others, such as Ruth Feldman and Daniel Messinger, have shown that synchrony between parents and babies occurs in behavior, heart rate, endocrine hormonal release, and brain activity.[63]

So what does this have to do with play? Play with your baby is synchrony, prolonged.

The Synchrony of *Play*

Let's go back to the vignette from the beginning of class. It was a small moment, less than a minute, but in that window, Ashleigh decided to turn her full attention to her baby and play. She consciously made a decision to prolong her synchronized interaction with her baby.

Play is *extended* synchronization with your baby that you do with intention. But that's not the whole story. It's also *fun*. It's not just engagement; it's positive engagement.

The defining elements of play with your baby are:

○ *Prolonged* synchrony
○ *Intention* to engage
○ *Positive* interaction

When you have these elements, your interaction is synchronous but feels separate from your normal stream of daily life.[64]

Why is play important for your baby? It's not just a boost in dopamine, which affects their well-being, it's also a lesson in social behavior.

Social School

Every time the bottle fell, Ashleigh made an "oh no!" face, which her baby thought was hysterical, and bent down to get it. That little game wasn't just silly; it was also teaching her baby that when we make mistakes we might feel frustrated or surprised or disappointed, but that it's OK. We can rectify the situation.

In your short and playful interactions, your baby is learning social skills. Ruth Feldman, a psychologist who has done extensive research on parent-infant synchrony, describes the benefits of play: "The high level of positive arousal that infants co-construct with their parents during the short daily episodes of face-to-face play, a level reached only during such shared moments, accelerates the maturation of the infant's relational skills and provides essential environmental inputs for the development of self-regulation and social fittedness."[65]

Babies aren't the only ones who learn social skills through play; animals do too. According to Nathan H. Lents, who wrote the book *Beastly Behavior*, one of the main reasons animals engage in play is to learn social rules. Imagine two elephant calves gently butting heads and wrapping their trunks around each other. They're not playing for survival needs, to get food, or to be more protected by their parents. Rather, they're playing to learn social behavior—the limits of interactions and reconciliation.[66]

Laughter Means Learning

Besides play being good for your bonding and for teaching your baby social skills, it's also beneficial for your baby's cognitive development.

A study showed that babies who laughed as they learned how to do a task were better at doing it later than those who didn't.[67] It's the same for adults. Do you tend to remember news that you heard on a funny late-night show more accurately than news you read online or in the paper? That's because laughter enhances our attention and recall.

Now's the Time

Maybe you're thinking, *No problem! I'll play with my baby when they can really engage with me.* But dear parent, *now* is the time to start developing your language of play with your baby. They're ready. And it will be a bonding booster. You can synchronize naturally all day (and you do!), but it's *play* that will make you both smile as you think of each other.

The play you do now with your baby will look similar in many ways to how you'll play with them when they're older. For instance, sometimes when my middle son giggles, I immediately remember the way he laughed when I hid behind the couch and popped out. His humor was very physical, in a slap-stick kind of way. And when my eldest and I are amused by something, we need only glance at each other with a smirk, similar to how he'd react to my bids for play when he was a baby. His humor has always been more understated, which has now turned into cynical humor.

The Game of All Ages

OK, let's get practical about how you can make this happen.

There's really only one type of game you need. You'll be playing versions of it whether your baby is three months, nine months, two years, or eight years old. It will get more sophisticated, but the foundation will be the same.

It comes down to action, response, and the space in between.

Do you ever make some sort of sound or gesture to make your baby smile? And then your baby laughs and you do it again? And again? Until your baby or you lose interest? That's what we're talking about, with a few tweaks. We're about to make it even more exciting and engaging for you both.

It Starts with Repetition

"One thing I do often with Lilah is that when it's time for a feeding, I repeat the same thing often. I ask her, 'Are you hungry? Are you so hungry? Are you the hungriest girl in the world?' In baby talk, of course. I phrase it the same way every time, and I swear she knows what I'm saying, and it's part of our bond. She's usually smiling or giggling." (Rachel, mom of Lilah)

Do you do something similar to what Rachel describes? You say something to your baby, then say it again and again.

Your baby learns through repetition. After only two times of you doing something, your baby learns to expect it again. Just like the scientist, gathering data on the patterns around them.

Your baby registers every slight change you make, and you, in turn, are sensitive to their quality of attention. Without realizing it, when you sense your baby's interest waning, you add something slightly novel. That balance between the familiar and new is a perfect setting for your baby's cognitive growth.

When parents do this type of repetition with their baby, they often do an action, get a response from their baby, and immediately do it again. But they might be missing out on an opportunity to deepen their engagement even more. It occurs in the *inaction*, not in the action. What happens *between* the repetitions?

The Tickle Monster Effect

Imagine this: You're hanging out with an eight-year-old and you raise your hands and start wiggling your fingers. What does the kid do? They giggle and run! They know the universal signal for the tickle monster when they see it.

What are they excited about? Not the tickling itself. That can often be uncomfortable or even painful. Rather, it's the *anticipation* of it that makes the tickle monster so much fun. And the anticipation happens in the pause.

Your baby is the same way. When you repeat a sound or action, they eventually expect it, and their delight comes in knowing you might do it again. In a world where they are picked up and put down, moved from here to there, and changed often without warning, knowing what the near future holds gives them an opportunity to feel some *control*. It's a moment of "baby therapy."

When you add a pause into the mix, you're giving your baby a minute to know what's next and sit with that excitement. It's just like the kids with the tickle monster.

The *Pause* Is a Gold Mine

The pause between each vocalization or gesture you make is a precious moment for you both. Here's what happens in that pause.

For your baby, the pause is what makes the game fun. It creates:

○ **Excitement!** Your baby feels the excitement of anticipation. They can hardly wait for it to happen again.
○ **Satisfaction.** The pause extends a rare moment of your baby feeling in control. It's empowering.

For you, the pause is a gold mine. In that mere moment you have an opportunity to learn about your baby's personality and shift your relationship from entertainer/audience to playmates.

When you take a minute to draw out the pause before repeating your gesture, you have a chance to learn about your baby's personality. How do they behave during the pause? Do they lie or sit absolutely still and stare at you like my son did when he was completely engaged in something? Or do they kick and giggle like my other son would do? Perhaps they let out a noise. Your baby's behavior during the pause tells who they are and how they behave when they're excited.

For instance, my eldest son would remain quite motionless, looking into my eyes while waiting for me to do my gesture again. Now, years later, I can still see that same intensity when he is waiting for something to happen.

Your Playmate

Remember Nicole from the quote at the start of this chapter? Here's how she continued: "Once I started playing in the way we learned in class with Amari, I realized she could actually play with me! She gets so excited when I wait for a second and look at her. She smiles and kicks her legs like crazy. I taught it to my husband,

and he loves doing it too. Amari can really play with us now. Makes me excited to play more games with her when she grows."

Playing this game was a turning point for Nicole in her relationship with her baby. Through this simple exchange she found that they could actually play together and both have fun.

This is significant. For many parents it's hard to relate to a baby during the first six months. They dismiss the baby as not sophisticated or interactive. But that's not the case. Once your baby is smiling, often after the first month, they're ready to get the joke.

In fact, in these simple interactions, your baby is learning how to make you laugh just as you are learning how to delight them. They are reading your subtle energy and receiving the message that you like when they make certain vocalizations or movements and maybe don't appreciate it as much when they do something else. They feed off the joy of connection when you are both smiling together and want to continue that as much as you do.

In fact, babies laugh more when there's someone nearby who gets the joke too. One study showed that when toddlers were watching a show with another toddler, they laughed eight times more than when they were watching alone.[68]

Caspar Addyman, who researches babies' laughter, believes that one of the reasons babies laugh is to reward *you* for prolonged attention. He found that babies laugh most when there is face-to-face interaction. So go ahead and let your baby gift you with their laughter. You won't be able to stop yourself from making it mutual.

How It Looks

Here's how this little game would look: You do a gesture of some sort, maybe a lip trill, kiss their belly, drop the bottle, or anything you're already doing.

Now do it again.

Now *pause* and look at your baby, who is now waiting for you to do it again. You hold their gaze with a look of anticipation, or the "anticipation face," as I call it. Then you do your gesture again. Pause. Repeat.

You do not need to have the perfect toy, invent Pinterest-worthy games, or channel your inner circus clown. That may elicit a big ol' eye roll in your current exhausted state.

Here's what you *do* need to do:

- **Be creative**—something you're already doing might be playful with a little flair.
- **Be open** to behaving a little silly and using gestures and sounds. Go crazy with high sounds, low sounds, facial expressions, gestures.
- **Use props** around you if they feel right.

The Dad Effect

For some parents, a game as simple as this can bring a dose of humanity to your baby. It may sound obvious to say that your baby is a person, but for many parents, it's hard to imagine their child with a capacity to understand the world around them.

Seeing yours as not just a baby who sucks your energy, time, sleep, and huge amounts of effort is a shift that makes parenting a lot more bearable. It helps you imagine a future of hanging out with your kid and laughing together about something.

Dads in our classes often talk about the shift they felt when they started playing this game with their baby. Not only were they excited to see their baby's response, but they felt like better parents—"I made my baby laugh!"

How the Game Develops
as Your Baby Grows

○ **Birth to 3 Months.** Your baby might look into your eyes and wait for you to do the gesture again.

○ **3 to 6 Months.** Your baby might kick legs, make a sound, make a noise, and show they are engaged and waiting in anticipation.

○ **6 to 10 Months.** Your baby might cue you to do the gesture again by making a sound or gesture themselves.

○ **10 to 15 Months.** Your baby might do the gesture themselves or even come up with a new one.

Bubble Moment: BABY FISH MOUTH*

♥ Make a noise and gesture. Best if it involves a sound and an action including touch. For instance, flutter your lips while making a sound and bring your head down to your baby's belly as you do it.

♥ Stop and look into your baby's eyes. Do the anticipation face—a look of surprise with your mouth slightly open and your eyes wide.

♥ Do your gesture and sound again.

♥ Pause again. Hold the pause.

♥ Do your gesture and sound again.

♥ Hold the pause even longer.

♥ Notice if your baby catches on to the game. Do they do a motion to show their anticipation? Do they even cue you to do your gesture again?

*Did you get the reference to *When Harry Met Sally*?

Play as a Magic Wand

When my son was eight he started writing a book he called *Parenting Mistakes through the Eyes of an Eight-Year-Old*. He presented his first chapter to me and declared that he would be turning it into a whole book. Clearly he had a lot of material.

The idea in the first two chapters (that's as far as he got) was a simple and essential message to parents of children of all ages: Parents need to be sillier, lighter, more fun.

> Babies and kids want to *play* and want us to be playful with them.

He said, "You ask me to get into the shower and then get upset when I don't go. But if you did it in a funny way, I'd probably do it." Then he had us roleplay so I could try different ways to make him laugh.

He reminded me of a lesson we all need to keep in mind *all* of the time as parents: Children want to have fun with us. They want to be silly and they want *us* to be silly. And this goes for *all* ages, from tiny babies to hormonal tweens.

You may be reading this and think, *I'm not worried about that! I'll win the shower battle because I'll teach my kid to do what I say.* But dear parent, you won't. Your child is inherently designed to avoid all serious tasks and veer toward fun instead. So, in the if you can't beat 'em, join 'em mentality, why not use play to your benefit?

We tend to be very serious in our very *important* adult world. We get caught up in day-to-day tasks that weigh us down. We work hard to get things done—to feed the kids, bathe them, make sure they're healthy, make sure we get our own stuff done. We get bogged down in a mode of checking things off our list . . . and forget to play.

And then, as our children grow, we get into the habit of trying to get through the daily rote tasks by going head-to-head with them. But as my son pointed out, we lose the battle.

Right When You *Least* Want To

Play can be a magic wand if you're able to rally right at that moment when you're having the most trouble—you're in your most tired, frustrated, state, and your baby is pushing back more than ever.

Your baby might seem tiny now, but one day in the very near future you might be trying to get your toddler's shoes on to get out the door. You'll be late to wherever you're going, your child will have demanded three outfit changes and thrown tantrums over lunch, and they will *not* want to put on shoes.

You'll just want it to end. A part of you will want to force the damn shoes on them and get going. But you'll also know that, if you do, there will probably be three more tantrums waiting around the corner.

You'll have no resources left. You'll feel depleted.

This is when you'll need to dig even deeper and find that playful place within you. How will you turn the moment into play?

You'll do a version of the tickle monster method. You'll put a sock on your hand, do something funny, then hide it behind your back. You'll do it again. Your baby will squeal with excitement, knowing the sock is about to come back out.

How Do You Make It Fun for *You*?

It comes down to connecting to how you had fun as a kid, letting yourself be silly. Funny faces, crazy dances, nonsensical songs, playing with a toy in a new way. As grown-ups, we don't call it play. When we give ourselves freedom to explore in an imaginative and inquisitive way, without a goal or solution in mind, we call it being *creative*.

Luckily for you, you've got your own personal creativity coach reminding you how it is to follow your instincts, hold off judgment when something feels ridiculous, and lead with lightness and curiosity. If you're a good student, you'll be able to reciprocate and help your baby continue to exercise, value, and enjoy their creative play.

Your baby can remind you how to *play* and reignite your creativity.

Important: It Has to Feel Authentic to You

For play to actually be fun for you and your baby, you're going to have to actually enjoy it. That means not playing in ways that don't feel comfortable.

Here's what I mean. My mother has never loved board games. Since she was a girl she always preferred imaginary play. Guess what she plays with the grandkids? Yup. Dolls and figures.

I don't love horseplay. My kids always want to wrestle and play-fight, and it's just not my cup of tea. On the other hand, I can play board games all day long.

Even with your baby, who might not be requesting a certain type of play with you, it's important that you enjoy it. Maybe you don't feel comfortable making funny faces. That's OK. You can find another way to be silly.

Maybe you don't like doing physical humor. That's OK. You can do more subtle humor with your baby, and believe me, eventually they'll catch on.

Also Important: It Has to Match Your Baby's Energy

I remember sitting at the airport with my baby on my lap, waiting for a flight on my way back to New York. The woman next to me immediately tried to engage him in play. She got a bit too close for my comfort and started moving his legs around and making whooping noises. Her energy was a lot. I felt my baby and I tense our bodies. I pretended he needed to nurse and turned away.

When I thought about this scenario later, I realized what had irked me. Not only was she a stranger invading our space and activating my protective mama bear instinct, but she also wasn't matching my son's energy.

If she had approached us in a more gentle way and had engaged him slowly and sensitively, noticing what he responds to and what he (and I) feels comfortable with, I would have actually felt grateful for her presence. I needed a break from him at that moment. Instead, she made us both stiffen and feel the opposite of playful.

When you're playing with your baby, remember the concept of synchrony. Take your time to notice your baby's energy, what sounds and gestures they respond to, what makes them scared, and what makes them curious.

Mary Ainsworth puts it nicely in her paper on attachment theory: "In play and social interaction, the mother who responds appropriately to her child, does not over-stimulate him by interacting in too intense, too vigorous, too prolonged or too exciting manner. She can perceive and accurately interpret the signs of over-excitement, undue tension, or incipient distress and shift the tempo or intensity before things have gone too far. Similarly, she is unlikely to under-stimulate the child, because she picks up and responds to the signals he gives when he is bored or when he wants more interaction than has heretofore been forthcoming."[69]

. . . .

Recap: WHY PLAY WITH YOUR BABY?

1. **Bonding.** Play is one of the best and quickest ways to have a meaningful Bubble Moment and feel super connected to your baby.
2. **To Get through Tough Moments.** Play will help you through tough parenting moments that may have you rolling your eyes and wishing time would go by a bit faster.
3. **Your Private Joke.** Play helps you communicate with your baby in a way that is only yours and your baby's. It's the feeling of having a secret or a private joke with someone that no one else knows about. And that private joke will be your way of interacting positively for years to come.
4. **Enriching.** Your baby learns social and cognitive skills through laughter and play.

Bubble Moment: PUPPET PLAY

💜 Put your hand in a puppet or sock, or hold a stuffy.

💜 Walk the puppet on your baby's legs, arms, and up to their face.

💜 Hold the puppet in front of them, then pretend the puppet is running away.

💜 Hide the puppet behind your back while doing the anticipation face.

💜 Bring the puppet back out and repeat.

💜 This can be done with their diaper if they're fussing during the change or with a ducky in the bath if they want to get out quickly.

9

Now You're Talking

IN THIS CHAPTER, YOU'LL LEARN HOW TO
ENCOURAGE YOUR BABY'S LANGUAGE
DEVELOPMENT THROUGH A FEW SIMPLE
BUBBLE MOMENTS.

I t's our sixth week of class and Jack, Henry's dad, shares how hard it's been for the past couple of weeks. Henry's sleep has been erratic, and he's been a lot fussier. Jack feels like he's running on empty and is barely getting through the day. "He might be teething, but who knows?" he says, exasperated and frustrated. "If only he could tell me what's wrong." And then he adds, "But if he could, would he say he wants ice cream for dinner every night?"

Rest assured your baby's adorable babbles and screechy howls will one day turn into well-articulated requests to stay at the playground for one more minute. But there may be more you can be doing to boost your baby's language today. As always in this book, the primary goal is to have more connected moments with your baby, and the secondary goal is to support and bolster their speech and cognitive development (and as we know, the first goal begets the second).

The Critical Period

You may think that language acquisition begins when your baby starts to say their first words, but it actually starts much earlier. In fact, one of the most important periods for their language development happens before their first birthday.

At birth, your baby is able to perceive the sounds of *all* world languages (about 600 constants and 200 vowels). I hate to say it, but you no longer have that ability. Adults can only discern the sounds of the languages they're used to speaking and hearing, not foreign languages. Your baby, however, is born with an open linguistic mind. That is, until they hit eight months or so.

Between 8 and 10 months, your baby prepares to learn the language they're going to speak in their culture. This short period is critical for their development. During this phase your baby gathers data on how often different sounds are used in the speech they hear around them. They develop an ability to differentiate between sounds used in their language and lose the ability to distinguish those that aren't.

Patricia Kuhl is a researcher whose fascinating studies teach us about early language and brain development. In one study, she looked at how babies in America and Japan perceive the sounds "ra" and "la." Between six and eight months, babies in both cultures recognized these sounds with the same frequency. But by 10 to 12 months, the American babies were much better at detecting the difference between these sounds than the Japanese babies. The reason is that those two sounds are frequently used in English but not in Japanese.

Kuhl discovered she could expose American babies to Mandarin during that two-month period and the babies would develop their ability to perceive sounds in Mandarin as well as babies who lived in Taiwan. Twelve lessons was all it took, even though they weren't immersed in the language and culture.

So what does your baby need during this critical period to support their development? *you.*

It Takes a Human

Kuhl wondered whether the American babies who learned Mandarin in two months were responding to a particular tutor or researcher. Would they learn as much if the lesson was presented on a TV? The answer was no.

Surprisingly, after 12 lessons in Mandarin viewed on screen, the American babies did *not* improve their Mandarin skills. Kuhl discovered that it only worked when a live person was speaking to them. That led her to understand an essential piece of the language acquisition puzzle: Social context plays a huge role in how babies absorb and discern sounds. For babies to learn language, they need to be in the presence of a human being engaging with them.

Babies need to be in the presence of a human being to learn language.

This is the case for two reasons:

1. **Gaze Shifting.** When babies in the study were with the live tutor, they actively shifted their gaze from the tutor's eyes to objects the tutor was referring to. It turns out that this type of engagement enhances phonetic learning.[70]
2. **Social Reward.** Babies are more motivated to learn in the presence of others when the other person is reacting to them in real time because it activates their reward system.[71] Your smiles, excitement, and delight when they grasp something new is contagious and gets them excited to learn more.

Kuhl and her team did a study that's going to make you cringe. Babies were hooked up to electromagnetic imaging while their mothers spoke to them for a few minutes, then looked at their phone for a while. Language areas of the brain that were activated when the mother directly engaged with the baby turned off when the mother looked at the phone. The signal flattened once again when the mothers turned to speak to someone else in the room. You'd think the baby would still be listening and absorbing language, even if they weren't directly engaged with it. Nope. They needed their mother to be attentive to them.

"The role of social cannot be underestimated. I think it will underpin all of human learning in a way that we've not understood before," Kuhl says. "Language is kind of a canonical case because it was thought to be so separate, not connected with cognition, not connected with social. We're turning that theory completely on its head."[72]

Once again, Kuhl's research shows us that it all comes down to your relationship with your baby.

OK, I'm a Human. What Do I Do?

Lucky for you, there are three actionable steps you can take to play while encouraging your baby's language development, and they can all be quality Bubble Moments. Let's break them down.

1. Mirror vocals
2. Sing your speech
3. Read in sounds

Before we get into these three approaches, let's go over two ground rules when it comes to communication with your baby.

SEIZE THE MOMENT

The best time to work on language with your baby is when they're babbling. Those cute sounds are a way for them to say, "I'm open for communication and ready to learn."

Parents often think they are like a French teacher facing a room of blank-staring students. But Rachel Albert, the director of the LVC Baby Lab at Pennsylvania's Lebanon Valley College, says that babies play a much more active role in their learning.[73] When they babble they're inviting learning. They guide your response through the *way* they babble and what they look at. And then it's a feedback loop—you respond to your baby, which influences how they react to you, and so on.

BE A GOOD CONVERSATIONALIST

How you respond can be like the difference between a fascinating conversation with someone at a party or an awkward exchange in a checkout line, and can encourage or discourage future bids for chatting. For instance, a vocal response that reacts to your baby's sounds can accelerate their phonological learning.[74] Even a silent but active response to their babbling, let's say when you touch them on the leg and smile at them, can encourage them to produce more speech-like vocalizations. However, a response that is mismatched—for instance, if your baby is playing with a cup and you are talking to them about a toy—can make it confusing for your little interlocutor and harder for them to learn.

Albert says, "When babies are babbling, they are more receptive to new information. Parents can take advantage of this by having conversations with their baby. And one rule of being a good conversationalist—stay attentive to what your partner is saying."

Babble Boost #1—
Vocal Mirroring

Have you ever noticed that you and your partner or you and your siblings have similar mannerisms? Maybe it's your tone of voice when you're being sarcastic or the way you slide your hands across a steering wheel. That's because you can't help but mirror each other's face, voice, body, and speech. The more we're with someone, the more we end up acting and sounding like them.

The "chameleon effect," as researchers call it, is the unconscious mimicking we do of the people around us.[75] It's human nature and acts like social glue, bonding us to each other and promoting group cohesion. In one study, participants who were paired with an actor who mimicked their behaviors (smiling, foot jiggling, and face rubbing) were significantly more likely to say they *liked* their partner (they didn't notice them behaving in a particular way) as opposed to those who weren't mimicked. Meaning not only do we instinctively mimic those around us, but we are attracted to people who do the same to us.

A similar experiment was done with six-month-old babies, and they seemed to feel the same way. The babies who were mimicked looked for longer, smiled more, and made more bids for interaction with adults who copied their gestures and facial expressions (such as swiping their hand across the table, making noises, or turning their head).[76]

You can bet that you and your baby are like chameleons, naturally mirroring each other throughout your day and bonding with every gesture. Your baby whines a bit, scowling with their eyebrows, and you say, "What's wrong, baby?" while making a pouty face and a pseudo-whiny voice. You open your arms to hug your baby, and your baby straightens their legs and waves their arms, mirroring your gesture to open your body to them.

Now let's take that a step further. Mirroring your baby's *vocal-izations* can have a huge role in their language development. When you mirror their sounds, you're conveying three important messages to your baby:

1. **I Hear You.** By repeating your baby's vocalization, you're acknowledging that you hear them and are giving them space to express themselves. This is more impactful than you think. It's exactly what encourages your baby to keep vocalizing.

   Babies are more likely to increase vocalizations when their caregiver responds immediately and directly to their sounds.[77] Makes sense—we'd all prefer to continue speaking with someone who seems like they're listening. The more your baby is encouraged to speak to you, the faster they'll learn how.

   As I sat here writing this, I saw a mom sitting across the café who was unconsciously mirroring her baby. He made a sound, and she immediately smiled and repeated back "ta ta." He looked at her for a while, smiling, and made another sound. He seemed to get a kick out of the fact that she made his sound.

2. **This Is the Sound You Made.** Repeating your baby's sound reflects their vocalization back to them and is a way to say, "You made this sound. I heard it and I can show you what it sounds like."

   Your baby is constantly learning your language by listening to you and listening to themselves make sounds. In fact, by 10 months, deaf babies who don't have the ability to hear you and themselves don't develop the ability to produce well-formed syllables as hearing babies do. By repeating their sound, you are helping your baby hear their own voice.

3. **We Can Have a Conversation.** When you mirror your baby's sound, you begin a call and response. They make a sound, you hear them, you make a sound back, etc. You're teaching them

the building blocks of communication and language. It only takes a couple of repetitions for your baby to catch on and maybe even launch into an elaborate conversation of turn-taking.

Even with nonsensical words, your conversation will look a lot like an adult conversation. One study with babies and caregivers showed that there was a similar pattern of switching pauses and accommodating for the other to "speak" in a very similar way you would talk with a friend.[78] Have you ever felt that way? If so, yes, your baby *can* have a conversation with you!

The more you mirror and respond to your baby's vocalizations, the more your baby will vocalize in response to you.[79] And then again, the more your baby vocalizes, the more you will respond. Research shows that both their frequent vocalizations and your responses will lead to increased language by 17 to 21 months.[80]

Stav, a mom in our classes who became a Baby in Tune instructor herself, explains how mirroring looks with her son:

"I mirrored Raz's babbles, but he didn't really respond at first. A month later I tried it again, and we had entire conversations! Now when we chat I mirror him and he also tries to make the sounds I make. I laugh when he does because it's so cute, and then he laughs, and then I laugh more."

HOW TO SPARK CONVERSATION

Sometimes a dialogue with your baby will happen organically. But you also might want to try igniting the chat. Here are some tips to getting it going:

Choose the Perfect Distance. Did you know that during the first few months, your baby's eyesight is still developing and the ideal distance for them to see is 8 to 10 inches, which, coincidentally, is the same distance from the breast (where they spend a lot of time) to your eyes? Nature amazes once again! It's partly why you may tend to have Bubble Moments when your baby is on the changing table. The distance is perfect, and you are attentive and available.

To start a conversation, stand over or in front of your baby at a distance that feels right for you both.

Communicate Readiness. When you're ready to have a conversation with your baby, start with eye contact. Then put your hands gently on their thighs or belly. Convey to your baby that you are fully present with them and are communicating through your face and body as well as voice.

Mirror *All* Sounds. Focus on the natural sounds your baby is making with their mouth—trills, exhales, clicks, growls. Mirror everything! Your baby will pick up on the fact that you are copying them and will increase their communication with you.

Read the Room. Maybe your baby doesn't feel like talking right now. That's OK! It's an opportunity to notice what they're doing instead. Are they looking to the side and avoiding your gaze? Maybe they're feeling tired or overstimulated. Are they looking into your eyes but not vocalizing? Great! That's communication. Your baby is engaged and interested.

Light the Spark. If your baby isn't vocalizing but you feel they're engaged and ready, try these techniques to suggest a vocal exchange:

○ **Unleash Your Inner Mariah Carey.** Make a very high vocalization, almost like a squeak, using the sound "ah." It grabs their attention, uses a sound they often use, and tells them you're ready to converse. Think of Mariah's whistle tone and go for that.
○ **Rev Your Engine.** What is the lowest sound your voice makes? If your baby doesn't respond to your high tones, a low growl

might do the trick. Emulate a tractor motor by engaging the back of your throat.

DON'T BE A CONVERSATION HOG

You're used to multitasking and quick thinking, but your baby is in what I call "baby time zone." Their thoughts happen so slowly that you can almost watch them in real time—*I'm holding my paci . . . I dropped my paci . . . Where is my paci?* (looking at their hand) *. . . There it is on the floor.*

Similarly, when you speak to another adult, the dialogue moves quickly. They speak, you speak, they speak, you speak, often without pauses in between. In fact, sometimes people show they're engaged by cutting in and speaking over the end of the other person's sentence before they've even finished. It's not out of rudeness or disinterest but out of involvement, excitement, and maybe an ants-in-our-pants need to keep things moving.

But since your baby thinks more slowly, pauses in conversation are necessary for them to integrate all the input around them.

I've seen parents reflexively fill the silence many times in class. Their baby makes a sound, they mirror it, and in the pause until their baby responds, they jump to fill the void by saying, "That's right, baby!" "Oh, I agree!" or "What else do you have to say?" It's not bad or harmful. In fact, in many instances it can be beneficial to your baby. It can be a perfect example of the necessary Parentese we'll talk about in the next section.

But this exercise is about something else. It's about letting your baby lead the conversation and you repeating their sounds and vocalizations *only*, without bringing in your language. If there is a moment of silence, it's an ideal time to see what your baby is doing, how they're looking at you, what sounds they're making from their mouth, what body movements or gestures they're making.

If, after a minute, your baby doesn't respond with another sound, you can try the conversation starter above. But most likely,

if you allow your baby space while giving them the
sense that you are attentive and attuned, they'll
come back with more to say.

Sometimes, especially after your baby hits
about eight months, your baby's vocalizations might turn into
monologues. In those cases, see if you can stay attentive and mirror the last part of their speech. You can also try following along
and mirroring them as they're speaking.

REALLY GO FOR IT

As we said, your baby is born with the ability to make all sounds
from all languages, and they love experimenting with their vocal
range. Your adult brain has undergone pruning, which means
that your synapses have grown in certain areas you need, like
speaking English or the language of your culture, and have been
disconnected in other areas that are not necessary to you. This is
your opportunity to reconnect to all those sounds you've lost along
the way. Try to mirror your baby vocally as precisely as you can,
no matter how silly it feels, including all of their many noises—
raspberries, lip trills, growls, squeaks, squawks, lilts.

Questions to Ask Yourself While Mirroring
Your Baby's Vocals

* Does my baby notice that I repeated their sound?
* How do they show their recognition?
* Do they babble more when I mirror them?
* Is their tone high? Low?
* Do they make sounds with their tongue and lips?

Babble Boost #2— Sing Your Speech

The second strategy for encouraging your baby's vocal communication is Parentese. Think about how you say the word "computer." We instinctively use the word all the time but don't think about all the musical elements that go into it. Most likely you put stress on the second syllable of the word, which creates a kind of melody. We start with a low note for "com"; we go up to a higher note on "pu"; and we end on a note that is lower than the first for "ter." We also syncopate this word, meaning we hold slightly longer on the middle syllable.

With our babies, we are even more musical with our speech. It's called Parentese. It's the sing-songy speech that we use with our babies across cultures.

Don't think you do it? Think again.

Even if you promised yourself before you had kids that you'd never use that high-pitched voice your Aunt Vivian uses when she bends over a stroller, you probably still do it. Don't worry, that's a good thing. Your baby actually prefers you to speak that way and stays more alert and engaged when you do.[81] The slower tempo and exaggerated melody and syncopation are like an invitation to your baby to learn.[82]

Parentese often follows the shape of a bell curve. You start low, go up high, and come back down. Think about how you might say "Hi" to your baby. It probably isn't a deadpan "Hi." It probably slides up and down, almost like a fire truck siren: "hiiiIIIiiii." Do you greet your partner when they come in the door like that? Nope. But you sure do when you see your baby again.

When you soothe your baby, you might be sing-songy too. Your voice might descend, starting higher and ending lower in tone. Think of how you might say, "It's OK," ending with a lower tone than you started. You probably even use that same descent when you're soothing a friend and saying, "I'm sorry that happened."

As it turns out, when you speak to your baby in Parentese, exaggerating your tone and stretching vowels, you're effectively cleaning up the language for your baby and making sounds more pronounced. This makes it easier for babies to do the sound mapping they need to do in order to learn the language. In fact, as you speak with those increased dynamics, the motor systems that control your baby's speech are activated in their brain. They're listening closely and getting ready to use that information for speaking.

Studies find that the more Parentese is used, by anyone in the home, the higher babies measure for language later.[83] This happens across languages and is a universal phenomenon.[84]

My oldest son's first word was "uh-oh." Can you guess why? Because we sort of sing it the same way every time we say it. Your baby is picking up on the *musicality* of language first and foremost.[85] There are a few reasons for this. One is repetition. Because we say "uh-oh" in the same melody each time, our babies can latch on to it and practice it. The second is dynamics. Your baby is looking for contrasting tones and becomes more alert when there are rises and falls in your speech.

HOW TO SING WHEN YOU SPEAK

1. **Keep Doing What You're Doing.** Most likely you're already speaking to your baby in a sing-songy way without even realizing it. Now that you're aware of it, you can accentuate it even more.

2. **Embody Your Inner Spanish Teacher.** Have you ever attended a language immersion class in which the teacher only speaks the new language—for instance, Spanish—throughout the entire class? They initially face a room of blank stares. And what do they do? Slow down their speech, accentuate their sounds,

simplify sentences, and label objects around them. Students of language immersion classes have been shown to outperform their peers in learning the language. Your baby's entire existence is like being in a language immersion classroom. So let's learn from the experts:

○ **Slow Down.** Speak slowly so your baby can pick up on the sounds of your words.
○ **Simplify.** Reduce some of your sentences to one or two words. This will help your baby pick up on the melody of the words without complicating things with the whole sentence.[86] You can say, "Eat banana?" before feeding or "stroller" when you are about to put them into the stroller.

3. **Notice the Hook.** You probably already say many words with a repeating melody. Notice them and accentuate them further. For instance, how do you normally say, "Let's go change your diaper!" Most likely there's a little melody to it. Go with it. Here's what Nadia said about noticing the hook with Naima: "I like to spend time every day getting close to my baby's face and saying 'hello' over and over, drawing the word out very slowly and exaggerating the mouth movements. We did this with our oldest, too, and they really try to mimic it back, straining hard with their mouth to make the same shape and getting out some verbal communication that sounds like a very early, rudimentary version of 'hello.' It's crazy how they can mimic! And how hard she's clearly working to get the sound out. It's so fun, definitely a bonding exercise." So keep on cooing, Aunt Vivian, you're bringing the baby one step closer to telling you that no, they don't like the ruffled dress you stuffed them into.

Babble Boost #3—
Read Into Sounds

The third strategy for encouraging your baby's speech is especially appropriate for babies who are a bit older. At around six months, your baby will start to gain more control over their sounds. Their vocalizations will take on more form and will include consonants and tones that mirror the melody in your speech.[87] Researchers call this "canonical speech." This is when you'll start to feel like your baby is almost speaking your language and has something clear to say, you just don't know what. The idea of this strategy is to pretend you do.

Gather clues to interpret their sounds by noticing what they're looking at, holding, or pointing to. Then respond to what you think they said—"Yes, that bird did just land on the tree."[88] Researchers found that when caregivers did this, their babies' language development was accelerated. The babies learned to restructure their babbling and incorporate phonological patterns from their caregiver's speech. They showed increased rates of consonant and vowel vocalizations, which eventually led to words, and were more likely to babble to their caregiver rather than just make sounds for the sake of babbling.[89] This happened only when caregivers responded "contingently," meaning as a direct reaction to their baby's vocalizations. The infants who were given noncontingent feedback did not develop language skills as rapidly.

When you respond to what you think your baby is saying, they feel that you're listening and because of that increase the amount of time they speak to you. You're telling them their sounds are effective. That leads to more interactions with you and more opportunities for learning.[90]

. . . .

Recap: THREE STRATEGIES FOR GOING FROM "WAH!" TO WORDS

1. Vocal mirroring
2. Sing your speech
3. Read into sounds

. . . .

Obviously, you can't and shouldn't be attentive to babbling all the time. Use these strategies for moments at a time whenever you can. They're powerful during this stage, when your baby is in their critical language-learning period.

Here is Jon's account of how mirroring went with Ben: "We did mirroring this week, and I couldn't believe I could actually have a conversation with Ben. He hasn't been so vocal, but this week he was chatting up a storm! I could suddenly imagine him older and us sitting watching a movie or going out to have dinner together."

Welcoming Words

As your baby nears the end of their first year, let's take this a step further and turn random sounds or babble into sounds with meaning. The secret to it? *Music.*

MUSIC FIRST, MEANING SECOND

My daughter's first word was *diaper*. But she didn't quite say *diaper*, with the *d* and *p* sounds. Rather, she said "ba pa." "Riiiiight," my husband said as he rolled his eyes, "of course that means *diaper*!" But I knew that's what she meant. How did I know? Because she *sang* the word. The melody was exactly the same as when I said the word.

Here's what I mean. Every time I was about to change her diaper,

Bubble Moment: VOCAL MIRROR

💜 Stand over or in front of your baby at a comfortable distance. The changing table is a perfect place for this.

💜 Look into their eyes and maintain eye contact for a while. Notice what your baby is doing. Put your hands on their legs or body to connect with them physically.

💜 Start to mirror the sounds they are making. It may not be vocalizations. It may just be opening and closing their mouth or exhaling. Mirror it all.

💜 If your baby isn't vocalizing, start to make very high sounds and very low sounds. The high sounds should sound squeaky; the low sounds can be a bit growly.

💜 Wait and see if your sounds elicit a conversation. If so, mirror your baby's sounds as precisely as you can.

💜 Allow for the pauses between your phrases and your baby's. Give your baby the confidence that there's no rush—you're waiting and are engaged and attentive.

💜 If there's no verbal back and forth, that's OK. Even just looking into each other's eyes and mirroring gestures and sounds is a conversation.

I would say, "Should we go change your diaper?" or "Do you have a dirty diaper?" And I always said the word *diaper* the same way—with a low pitch as I said "di" and popping up high with my pitch as I said "per."

When my daughter "said" it, she wasn't repeating the consonants of the word but, rather, the melody and rhythm. She was singing it. She said "ba pa" by lowering her pitch on "ba" and rising up high for "pa."

It turns out that she isn't the only one who learns language through music. Research shows that babies use melody, timbre, and rhythm to learn sound structure in speech and to distinguish their native language from others.[91] They're not just listening for the effect behind what is being said or to the meaning. Instead, they are focused on how language *sounds*.

There is growing evidence that babies show overlapping brain activation when they hear infant-directed speech or instrumental music, and that listening to language and music involves similar detection processes (this changes as they grow and process music and language in different parts of the brain).[93],[94]

"Without the ability to hear musically, we would be unable to learn language."[92]

You already sensed this. It's why you speak to your baby in Parentese, enhancing patterns of language by using a larger pitch range and more exaggerated melodic contours than typical adult-directed speech.[95] Your baby is listening to the rhythmic and phonemic patterns that you're accentuating. As if hearing a vocal performance, they're searching for consistencies in your melody, intonation, timbre, and rhythm.

It's almost as if you're teaching your baby your culture's birdsong. And in fact, researchers have found that babies learn language during their first year similarly to how songbirds learn their songs.[96] Overlapping brain areas show that, like the songbirds, your baby is listening closely to the song in your speech.

In their article titled "Music and Early Language Acquisition," Anthony Brandt, Molly Gebrian, and L. Robert Slevc argue that music holds a central place in language development. They write, "From a developmental perspective, the progression is clear: first we play with sounds; then we play with meanings and syntax. It is our innate musical intelligence that makes us capable of mastering speech."[97]

Have you ever heard it said that music is universal? Brandt, Gebrian, and Slevc suggest that perhaps we feel that way because music is closest to how we heard language in infancy, before syntax, vocabulary, and semantics took over.

So how can you use this information to help your baby? I'm glad you asked.

Four Ways to Help Your Baby Go from Music to Meaning

1. ACCENTUATE THE MUSIC

Emphasizing the music in your speech can help your baby learn words. My son's first word was *uh-oh* because we'd naturally always sing it, starting higher on the "uh" and dropping a few notes to say "oh." It's a very common first word because of that.

To accentuate the music in your speech, keep these three elements in mind:

Key Words. What are some words you often repeat during the day? You want your baby to learn the words that will be most useful to them. Examples of these are: more, no, want, sister, tired, and poopy. Say those words often in simple sentences and give them an extra tune.

If you're looking for a song with a bunch of common first words, my song "New Words" incorporates the classics—mama, dada, banana, up, down, more—and adds gestures to them.

Go Beyoncé on It. How do you usually say that key word? Most likely there is a melody that you do every time you say it to your baby. Once you notice it, it will be hard to ignore.

Now go big. Accentuate the melody and make it clear and simple. Think of it like a hook of a chorus. A good chorus is catchy because it's simple enough to be singable and original enough to distinguish it from all the other choruses out there.

Repeat, Repeat, Repeat. Music has a special trait that language doesn't have: The melody (usually) repeats. You can *say* "happy birthday to you" in many ways, accentuating different words and using a different rhythm structure each time. But when you *sing* "happy birthday to you" you sing it the same way every time. That's what makes it learnable. So sing your key words every chance you get. Let your baby learn the hook.

Basically, keep doing what you're doing, only do it even more. You are already speaking to your baby in a sing-songy way. Now take it a step further to help your baby latch on to specific words and begin to distinguish them from the music of your whole sentence.

2. INVOLVE ALL THE SENSES

People learn through four modalities: auditory, visual, kinesthetic, and tactile. Until a few years ago, it was thought that you could give children a questionnaire, find out their preferred learning mode, and gear the instruction toward the student's strength.[98] The idea was that if someone is more inclined to learn through visual stimulation, they will have greater success with a graph, drawing, or worksheet. On the other hand, if someone is a tactile learner, they'll prefer to touch and manipulate something, such as a globe, math blocks, or playdough letters.

We now know that it's extremely hard to parse out which modality would be best for each child. Therefore, the growing consensus among educators is that a multisensory approach is most beneficial.[99] To increase your baby's perception and attention, it's best to involve stimulation from all modalities.[100]

There just so happens to be a fun and easy way to teach your baby language that includes their auditory, visual, and sensory experience: hand gesture songs. Why hand gesture songs?

They Hit All Four. Hand gesture songs teach your baby through their auditory (singing), visual (they see your gestures), tactile (they mirror the gestures and you touch their hands), and kinesthetic (with songs that involve full body movements) elements. This gives your baby a chance to use their learning strength.

Melody Helps a Lot. Research shows that babies learn lyrics more easily when they're paired with a melody than when they're on their own.[101] They also learn melodies more easily when they're paired with lyrics. So when you're teaching your baby new words, keep singing! The pairing of words with song works magic.

Repetition. The genius of songs is that they repeat the same way. So when you add gestures to a familiar melody it gives your baby a chance to predict the gestures and learn the connection between the movement and the word. Imagine your baby's excitement knowing that you're about to sing "down came the rain and washed the spider out." The melody helps your baby remember which gesture to do and what word to sing.

Signs Add Meaning. By adding gestures to words, whether in a song or not, you are offering your baby another symbol besides a vocal sound. For instance, the gesture of closing fingers together on both hands and meeting both hands at the tips, which goes along with the word *more*, teaches your baby that that motion means something and can help them communicate their needs. Gestures that go with words help your baby learn the concept of referential communication.[102]

It's Fun. We already know that music boosts mood, lowers stress, and gets you in sync with your baby. Why is "The Itsy Bitsy Spider" the number one all-time favorite children's song? Because it's fun to do. Your baby loves watching you manipulate your fingers and trying to do it themselves with their little fingers. It's much more interesting than simply speaking to them or singing without gestures.

It's Bonding. As you sing a hand gesture song, your baby shifts their gaze from your eyes to your mouth and your hands. As we saw in the last section, the fact that your baby follows your gaze and raises their eyes to you helps them learn and keeps them engaged and connected with you. And that makes it a perfect Bubble Moment!

Pro Tip: To make your hand gesture songs even more educational and engaging to your baby, take a tip from how deaf parents communicate with their babies.

Remember how we said that Parentese accentuates the melody in your speech? It effectively cleans up your words so your baby can tune in to the tone and rhythm. Well, it turns out that deaf parents also do a form of Parentese, but it's with *movement* instead of vocals.[103] When deaf parents communicate with their baby, they modify their signs to be more simple, slow, repetitive, and exaggerated.

We can learn from that.

As you gesture a spider, rain, bunny, or ocean, go big with your gestures. Open your fingers to their full capacity and then close them shut, swing your arms out wide, add facial expressions to go with your movements. Basically, *go big*. The more you do, the easier it will be for your baby to learn your gestures just like they learn your sounds.

---

3. READ WITH MELODY

As I'm sure you've heard before, reading to your baby is extremely beneficial. It has been shown to increase their vocabulary by three years, and that advantage remains present years later.[104] Studies show that infants as young as eight months old begin learning words that frequently occur in storybooks read to them.[105]

But there's a secret ingredient to this that helps your baby learn the words in the story even more—repetition. It turns out that reading that same book to your baby over and over is the secret sauce that helps them learn the words in the story.[106]

Do you have a theory on why that might be? I do. Music.

My baby loved *Brown Bear*. Every time I read it he'd read it with me. But he didn't quite say the words; rather, he'd sing the *melody*.

Huh? It's not a song, it's a book.

That's true. But once you're on your 49th reading of the same book, you tend to not just *say* it; you *chant* it. You've become so accustomed to the sequence, phrasing, and rhyme of the sentences on each page that they fall into a similar melodic pattern and rhythm.

Think of how you might say:

Brown bear, brown bear, what do you see?
I see a red bird, looking at me.
Red bird, red bird, what do you see?
I see a yellow duck, looking at me.

Do you almost sing the words, rising and falling with the tone of your voice? For instance, you might say "brown" a little higher than "bear" and end the sentence on an even higher note with "see." Then you might say "I" in an even higher tone than the rest to accentuate it.

When I would read this to my baby he'd say along with me, "ba ba ba ba wa wa see?" He wasn't quite saying the words, but he was marking the lyrics in the melody. He got the tune of it and many of the consonants. And while he sang it with me he'd look at the pictures and associate them with the words he was saying. Soon after, his pronunciation of those same words improved and sounded more like the actual words.

Reading the same book to your baby and accentuating the music of it helps your baby predict the words in the melody and connect the pictures they see with the words they hear.

So the next time your baby wants you to read the same book for the 539th time, do it with gusto! Besides the benefit of improving your baby's vocabulary, it's also a very effective way to ease your baby into bedtime, bond with them over a calming and enjoyable Bubble Moment, and get some quality time while you relax too.

Tips to Getting an A+ at Reading to Your Baby

⭐ **Sing It.** Notice the chant you might be doing already, especially with rhyming books, and go with it. Books can be like a song.

⭐ **Let Go.** Does your baby like to skip pages? Flip back? That's OK! For your baby, the story is not necessarily linear. That's something we teach them as they grow. For now, they're simply enjoying the physicality of the book, the pictures, the melody of it, and being with you. Eventually they'll want to read from beginning to end. But if they're not there yet, let it go. Enjoy your baby's refreshing perspective that there is no end game. That's our thing.

⭐ **Take Your Time.** Let your baby point to things, pause on certain pages, look around the room if they're distracted, look at you, and interact with you. More important than getting through the book is the bonding. If your reading session only includes your baby pointing out pictures on *one* page, that's great. You've both spent some time with joint attention, and your baby has shown you their perspective.

⭐ **Play the Part.** Even a book like *Goodnight Moon* can inspire some acting. Use voices to make it interesting. Through your acting your baby will start to understand the idea that the pictures in the book represent characters with stories.

* **Show Emotions.** As the characters start to have more complicated emotions, like sadness, anger, or disappointment,
exaggerate them. Your baby is learning a lot about emotions by watching you pretend to have difficult feelings in a
safe environment.
* **Leave Blanks.** As your baby gets older, start asking questions—
"What's that?" Or let them fill in the end of a sentence they
know. Why might they know the last word? Because it's
like a song!

I've got some good news for you. It turns out that not only does
reading to your baby boost their language development, but it's
also good for you. In a study with over 2,000 parents, reading to
babies predicted less harsh parenting at five years. The researchers believe that shared reading contributes an important aspect to
the relationship that may lead to better behaved kids (and probably
more attuned parents).[107]

It's possible that the parents who naturally read to their babies
already parent less harshly. But in this chicken or egg scenario, since
there are huge benefits to reading as is, it's worth giving it a shot.
Who knows? Maybe having a calming Bubble Moment reading to
your baby every night is like a meditation that relaxes you both.

4. MAKE SOME MUSIC

Here's your final tip for going from babbling to blabbing: Sing,
bounce, dance, and play drums with your baby. Studies show that
playing music at home with your baby can affect their language
development.[108]

In one study parents did a variety of music activities with their
baby at home—they bounced with their babies on fitness balls to
the music, beat out the rhythms they heard on drums, played

freeze dance, and shook rattles to the beat. After six weeks of this training, babies showed a shift in brain processing and went on to develop stronger language skills when they were 12 months old.[109] That's a huge lasting effect!

In addition, Kuhl found in her lab that 12 weeks of a musical social intervention with 9-month-olds increased their speech and language acquisition. Kuhl believes that the intervention "enhanced infants' ability to extract temporal structure information and to predict future events in time, a skill affecting both music and speech processing."[110]

Creating Your Own Language

The best part of your baby starting to grasp language is the opportunity to develop your shared language together. You can learn so much about your baby as they begin to communicate with you. What words do they latch on to? It's an opportunity to learn what excites them and how they see the world.

Final word: Those adorable mistakes your baby makes as they learn language are precious. Take the time to video them learning how to talk, using their own sounds, and making sense of the world. My daughter used to say "chuch it" for touch it. We all still say that sometimes because it became part of our family language.

This is the time for your baby to learn your language and for you to learn your language anew.

Bubble Moment: SING AND SIGN

💜 Put your baby on a blanket in front of you, sitting on your lap facing you, or in a high chair or stroller.

💜 Sing a song with gestures. A list follows.

💜 The best songs involve hand gestures and touch as well.

💜 As you sing, look into your baby's eyes and at your hands. Show your baby the gestures you are making.

💜 Make your gestures as big as you can. Open your hand wide, move your fingers to their full motion.

💜 Repeat your songs often. Let your baby learn the words and the gestures and be able to predict what's coming in the song.

Hand Gesture Song Ideas

"Where Is Thumbkin?"

"The Wheels on the Bus"

"Head, Shoulders, Knees, and Toes"

"Little Bunny Foo Foo"

"The Itsy Bitsy Spider"

"Patty Cake"

"There Was a Little Turtle"

"I'm a Little Teapot"

"The Ants Go Marching"

"Hey Diddle Diddle"

"Open Shut Them"

"If You're Happy and You Know It"

"Jig Jog"

"Five Little Monkeys"

"Five Little Ducks"

"Peace Like a River"

"Do Your Ears Hang Low?"

"Baby Shark"

"The Hokey Pokey" by Charles Mack, Taft Baker, and Larry Laprise

"Skidamarink" by Felix F. Feist and Al Piantadosi

"Tony Chestnut" by The Learning Station

"Grey Squirrel" by The Learning Station

continued

"One Fine Face" by
    Sesame Street
"Hands Up (Give Me Your
    Heart)" by Ottawan

"Coconut" by Harry
    Nilsson

Vered's Songs

"Bikeride"

"Galloping Horse"

"New Words"

"Rocking in the Boat"

"Flying Hands"

"Tummy Time Song"

PART 4

THE
REMEDY
TO
ROUTINE

10

Sound Sleep Habits

IN THIS CHAPTER, YOU'LL LEARN HOW
A LULLABY CAN MAKE YOUR DREAMS
COME TRUE.

It's the end of our seventh class and, as usual, we're singing the "Sleep" song. The parents cradle their babies in their arms and give them bottles and pacis. The babies know the drill, and everyone, including the parents, seems excited about the prospect of rest.

As we sing, I remind the parents to breathe in deep between phrases to relax their body and voice. We all slow down and sway with the rhythm of the of the song:

Sleep my baby, sleep my baby

ME: "Deep breath in."

Sleep my baby, sleep my baby

ME: "Relax your shoulders, take a deep breath in."

The babies snuggle in closer. I see a few of the parents signaling to each other with huge smiles that their baby fell asleep.

The Preschool Teacher Technique

Question: What does a preschool teacher do when she wants the kids to clean up the blocks or crayons so they can move on to another activity? Do you know what it is?

She sings the "Clean Up" song (originally sung by Barney, an anthropomorphic purple dinosaur). If you've ever been in a preschool or daycare class when this happens, you've probably seen the kids pick up their heads, stop what they're doing, and start cleaning. They almost turn into robots programmed to put away their toys and sing along.

Why does this song work so well? How does it get the kids to stop what they're doing and start cleaning?

It goes back to a discovery made in the 1890s by a physiologist named Ivan Petrovich Pavlov.

Pavlov's Dogs

When studying the digestive response of dogs, Pavlov noticed something interesting. The dogs salivated even before they received food, when they heard the assistant approaching.

Pavlov set out to explore this further and made a discovery that continues to inform the field of psychology and is taught in every Psych 101 class.

In his study, Pavlov rang a bell and then gave his dogs food. For the next feeding he did the same—rang the bell and then gave the food. Same for the next and so on. Eventually, the dogs salivated just at the sound of the bell, even before they got the food. They associated the sound of the bell with receiving food and had a *physiological* response when they heard it.

So what happened? The dogs became **conditioned** to the sound of the bell. Classic conditioning is when an automatic response (like salivating) is paired with a stimulus (like a bell). The dogs in Pavlov's study became conditioned because the stimulus was:

○ **Identifiable.** The sound of the bell was unique and the dogs could recognize it.
○ **Repeated.** Pavlov always used the same sound.
○ **Consistent.** Before every meal, Pavlov rang the bell.

Your Baby as the Dog

Your baby is like a dog. In fact, we all are! We're all conditioned to many things without even realizing it. For instance, do you wake up and have coffee? If so, you've probably learned to associate your morning with a cup of coffee (and perhaps the need for caffeine).

When I was pregnant with my first, I felt extremely nauseous. During that time, I used a body soap that had a lavender scent. Now, whenever I get a whiff of a similar smell, I have a physical reaction. I'm immediately flooded with the sensations that went along with nausea.

This is good news when it comes to your baby. It means you can intentionally reinforce a desired behavior of your baby with a stimulus if they are paired together. (It also means negative behaviors can be cemented easily, but let's focus on the positive ones for now.)

In one study, pacifiers were hooked up to speakers that would play the mother's voice when the baby sucked on it.[III] The infants quickly learned the connection and increased sucking in order to hear their mother's voice. Meaning their sucking was reinforced as a result of the reward they received. It was used as a medical intervention because improving

Conditioning can help with one of your biggest struggles—*sleep.*

their sucking increased feeding and weight gain, leading to shorter hospital stays.

Our propensity to learn behavior paired with reinforcement even happens in vitro. One study showed that fetuses increased kicking to hear their father's voice and feel touch through the belly.[112]

So what's the best place to use conditioning with your baby? For one of your biggest challenges—*sleep*.

Conditioning to the rescue! Your stimulus has the potential not just to elicit a behavior like going to sleep—it can also relax your baby and increase your bonding.

Let's Go Lullaby!

"For a while I didn't feel comfortable singing with my baby. I just don't have a good voice. But after this class I tried doing it more. My baby really responded to it. At first she seemed to just like the sound of my voice, but now I think she's used to it and actually gets more tired when she hears it. Every time I sing it she starts rubbing her nose." (Kayla, mom of Isla)

There's a reason lullabies are sung in cultures across the world through generations.[113] They actually work and can make your bedtime and nap routine much easier. Lullabies are the ideal stimulus to pair with sleep and cue your baby for sleep.

These are the behaviors many parents report their baby doing when they sing their lullaby every time they put their baby down:

○ Eye rubbing
○ Yawning
○ Nose rubbing
○ Ear pulling
○ Eyes closing

The other day I got an email from a mom who wrote: "Vered, we've been singing your sleep song for my baby since we took your class. Now, incredibly, Alma is so obsessed with 'Sleep My Baby' that it literally has a hypnotic effect on her—we put it on (on Spotify, often in the car) and she instantly chills out and falls asleep. I wanted to reach out to you because we just got back from an adventurous trip to the north coast of the Dominican Republic, where we played 'Sleep My Baby' . . . in a cave at Alma's request so she could nap in her carrier. I had to write and tell you because this song has become *so* special and important to our family."

Why Is a Lullaby the Perfect Cue?

Ah, so many reasons. Let's go through them.

THE HOOK

A song repeats the same way every time. Without a lullaby you might say, "OK baby, time to sleep now," or "Let's go to bed, sweet baby," each night a little differently. But a song will always have the same melody and lyrics. This makes it an "identifiable stimulus," just like the bell.

Your baby loves repetition. It's comforting and helps them learn. Within a month your baby will know your song and will have a physiological response when they hear it.

IT'S INHERENTLY SOOTHING

Has this ever happened to you? You're feeling a bit stressed, you've spent a good portion of your day focusing on your to-do list. You get in the car and a song comes on the radio. Suddenly you're noticing how pretty the sun looks on the trees, you're thinking about how much you love your baby, you're singing along to the song.

Music is powerful in so many ways. Not only does it calm us, but it makes us take a step back and widen our lens from the minutiae of our lives to the big picture. And once we're there, we feel more grateful and at ease.

Lullabies have the power to soothe your baby and *you*. They help you both wind down. This is key. As we said in Chapter 6, it's all about you. Having a routine that slows you down and makes you take in deep breaths is just as beneficial for you as it is for your baby.[114]

For your baby, a song can help smooth the transition from being awake to sleep and help them relax their body through it. Lullabies have been shown to lower heart rate in babies, improve feeding patterns and sucking patterns, increase oxygen saturation, and decrease stress behaviors.[115],[116]

Not only that, but singing while you're *pregnant* can also have an effect on your baby's behavior post-birth. One study showed that babies who were sung to in utero cried less after they were born.[117] Wow!

EXPECTING WHAT'S TO COME

A lullaby cues your baby for what's to come not only physically but mentally. The more they hear it, they come to understand that it leads to being put to sleep.

As your baby grows, they develop "symbolic function," which is the ability to create mental images of objects that are not immediately in front of them. Meaning a picture of a banana will make them think of an actual banana.

When you sing your familiar lullaby, the song begins to act like a symbol. Your baby develops the capacity to hear the song and imagine going to sleep in their crib. The lullaby will help them mentally prepare for what is about to happen.

This is important. Your baby might not be able to use the lullaby as a mental cue quite yet, but soon enough they will, and it will be

right at the moment when they absolutely do *not* want to stop playing to go to sleep. The lullaby will help them gain a sense of control.
They'll hear it and be able to mentally prepare for what's to come.

AN EMOTIONAL TRANSITIONAL OBJECT

The term *transitional object* was first coined in 1951 by Donald Winnicott to describe an object like a lovey or blanket that a child develops an attachment to. Here's how it works: At first your baby needs
you to soothe them when they're dysregulated. But with time, they
may begin to soothe themselves with an object, or a lovey, in your
absence. A transitional object helps them shift from being soothed
solely by you to finding other ways to soothe themselves.

How does this relate to lullabies?

Have you ever heard a song you used to sing with a friend, or
your wedding song, or a religious song, and it makes you think
of the people you were with when you heard it? Not only that, it
makes you *feel* the feeling of being with the people you associate
with the song? Maybe it's happy, or loved, or angry, or supported.

When you sing your lullaby with your baby at night, you're
infusing the song with lots of feelings—being cuddled, feeling loved, relaxed, warm. Every night
those feelings get extra baked into the
song. Then, when they hear the song and
you're not around, all those feelings come
flooding back. They may even see you in
their imagination, depending on how
old they are.

> The more you sing
> your lullaby, it becomes
> infused with the feeling
> of your connection with
> your baby.

This is useful. It means that when you leave your baby with
Grandma, at daycare, or with a nanny, you can ask them to sing
the lullaby. When they do, it will elicit the deep feelings of safety
and connection you and your baby feel together. Thus, it's an emotional "transitional object" that helps them transition from being
soothed by you to being soothed by others.

THE PERFECT BUBBLE MOMENT

Tell me if this sounds familiar: "I work full time and feel like I barely have time with my baby. When I am finally with her, I'm so exhausted I just want her to go to sleep. I feel so guilty about it. But then, when she's finally sleeping, I spend the whole evening looking at pictures of her on my phone and showing them to my partner." (Ori, dad of Sophie)

Have you felt the way Ori does? I have. You've been at work all day and are exhausted. Or maybe you've been with your baby all day and desperately need a break. The last thing you want to do is sing a lullaby. You just want the baby to go to sleep *now*.

But hold on one more minute if you can, parent. The lullaby before bed is a *prime* Bubble Moment opportunity. If you're able to slow down the last few minutes before freedom, you'll reap benefits not only for your baby's sleep (which means for you) but for your relationship.

The lullaby is a time for you both to pause, connect, look into each other's eyes. Then your baby falls asleep with the experience of feeling tenderly loved and safe in your arms. Same for you. It makes you feel more connected to them than other types of social interaction and even makes you feel happier.[118]

Remember entrainment from the rhythm chapter? Singing to your baby also synchronizes visual interactions between you and your baby, which increases your bonding.[119]

Why does Ori finally get his baby down but then look at pictures of her on his phone? Or peek in on her sleeping? Or look at the monitor? Because separation from our baby is as hard for us as it is for the baby. Singing a lullaby is a way to intensely connect before that separation. If you're able to do that, you'll put them down with a feeling of gratification and will be able to hit Netflix without the extra guilt.

It's basically the concept of "work hard, play hard." Connect hard with your baby so you can rest hard when you're *not* with your baby. Be present with your baby before bed so that you can then feel more present with your partner, friend, book, show, self.

. . . .

Recap: WHY A LULLABY MAKES BEDTIME AND NAPS SO MUCH EASIER

1. Physical cue
2. Mental cue
3. Songs are soothing
4. The ultimate Bubble Moment
5. Emotional transitional object

Convinced? Good. Now let's make it happen.

. . . .

Which Lullaby Should I Use?

Any song can be turned into a lullaby. The characteristics of a lullaby are that they have longer notes, are sung slowly, and often have a simple melody. But any song can work. One mom in my class liked to sing a slowed-down version of "Sweet Child o' Mine."

For a list of lullabies that parents have told me they use over the years, go to www.babyintune.com/lullabykitparents.

THE BEST LULLABY OF ALL

Parents, I can give you the most wonderful lullabies that were ever written, but there's one that will be the most effective by far.

It's the lullaby that's personal to *you*. Here's how you know your lullaby is personal:

It's a Family Tune. Maybe your grandmother sang it to your parents. Maybe your aunt told you about it. Start asking the elders in your family questions—was there a lullaby that was sung to you?

Here's what Maria said: "I don't speak Spanish very well like my grandmother and parents, but I sing a song in Spanish that my mother sang to me. When I do, it feels like Valentino and I are both connecting to our larger family."

It's Your Creation. When I had my first baby, I didn't intend to write a lullaby. It just happened. If you listen to it, you'll hear how simple it is:

Sleep my baby
Sleep my baby
Close your eyes
Close your eyes
I'll see you in the morning
When the night has come
I'll be here my darling
To keep you safe and warm

I basically sang what I wanted to happen. I really wanted my baby to go to sleep and close his eyes. I also needed us both to know that we'd see each other in the morning. There was no reason at all to wake up at night! (Well, I had to try.)

Writing a lullaby with your baby is easier than you think. In the next chapter I'll give you a short songwriting lesson so you can start writing your own personal repertoire with your baby.

The songs you write with them now will be the same ones they remember when they're in college telling their friends about it, or when they have their baby and hear your voice in their head.

Do I Need to *Sing* the Lullaby?

Parents in my classes often tell their stories of long drives on the highway. Baby starts to fuss, fussing escalates to crying. Baby doesn't want a bottle, they can't pull over to feed, baby throws away paci and toys. They put on music and the baby is instantly soothed.

(In their stories it's always my music, but that has yet to be scientifically proven.)

There is no doubt that music has the power to soothe babies, and *us*, whether it's sung or prerecorded, but is singing more effective than hearing it on speakers?

It turns out that it's not an overwhelming advantage, but live singing does seem to win the prize and results in deeper sleep for preterm infants.[120]

One study shows why that might be the case: Babies remain calm for twice the amount of time when they heard a recording of music versus a recording of *speech*.[121] Music recording won over speech in that study but wasn't compared with live singing.

We also know that babies prefer to hear their parents sing *a cappella*, without being accompanied by instruments.[122] That means they prefer your voice alone compared with your voice with other sounds. This isn't a direct answer to our question but is significant because recorded music often has instruments accompanying the vocals.

But here's the most important part: When you sing to your baby, you modify your voice and dynamics based on your sweet audience of one.

Studies show that when parents sing directly to their babies, their singing is slower, more energetic, and has more pitch variability and exaggerated rhythm.[123]

Why do we do this? Because we want to attract our baby's attention and communicate different emotional messages. We alter our voice to fit our baby's mood, physical state, and age. We change subtle elements of our voice and rhythm to match our baby in that particular moment.

But even more importantly, infant-directed singing is more *emotional*.[124] When parents sing to their baby, they soften their tone and are more expressive. Your baby feels it. Imagine standing in the audience when your favorite rock star catches your eye and sings the next line looking at you. Your baby feels the connection when you, their favorite rock star, sings to them. Does recorded music do that? Nope.

Singing to your baby is a connection slam dunk. It's a Bubble Moment maker.

So who is our winner?

I think you knew from the start. *Live singing*. But not by a ton. Which means that if you don't want to sing, that's OK. Playing a lullaby through the speakers on a consistent basis will still help your baby go to sleep.

Tips to Help You Seal the Deal

Tell me if you relate. You sing a lullaby, give your baby the last feed, and prepare everything for a perfect landing into the crib. Your baby is drowsy and falls asleep instantly. You're doing an internal happy dance because me time is just around the corner. You taper your song a bit and walk out.

Two minutes later? Ugh. Your baby starts to cry. This was basically the entire first year with my eldest. I realized that the only way to truly ease him into sleep was by using . . .

THE FADE-OUT

It's a technique musicians have been using forever. Basically it means gradually lowering the volume, But it's easier said than done.

Have you ever ridden a horse? When you take them out on a trail, on the way out they may meander, munch plants from the side of the trail, and have an easy pace if left to their own devices. But the way back is a different story. Especially as they approach their barn, where they know rest and food await, they pick up the speed. In fact, for those last 20 minutes they almost instinctively trot. They just want to get home.

We're kind of like that. We might have taken a lot of care preparing our baby for bed, but once the end is in sight we may start to rush it. Of course, your baby senses your quickening, just like you might sense the urgency of the horse who wants to get home quickly and is a little clumsier with his steps.

The Fade-Out is crucial in those moments. Here's why:

For You. It forces you to slow down and be more intentional during those last few minutes. If you're able to reduce stress and your energy level, your baby will too. It also forces you to be present. It's almost impossible to fade out without being fully present while you're doing it. For instance, it takes a lot of vocal control to taper out the volume. Although freedom calls, your concentration will keep you in the moment.

For Baby. It eases the transition. Think about when you're listening to a song on your headphones. Many of the songs fade out to slide you into the next song. The Fade-Out that you will do with your own voice will help your baby transition from noise, togetherness, and excitement into sleep.

How to Do a Successful Fade-Out at Bedtime

* Give yourself two extra minutes to do this.
* Imagine you have two dials on your singing—one makes the song increasingly *slower* and one makes it increasingly *softer* in volume.

continued

✽ As you sing your lullaby, start to hold out the notes longer and let your voice be more relaxed and more sleepy.

✽ Increasingly allow your voice to get softer and softer, approaching a whispery tone. Turn that volume knob down slooooooooowly.

Bubble Moment: THE FADE-OUT

💜 Hold your baby as you sing them your lullaby.

💜 As you sense your baby getting sleepy, start to hold each note longer, making the song slower.

💜 Gently put them down in their bed as you're singing slowly.

💜 Start to reduce volume ever so slightly. This can take a few minutes.

💜 As you reduce volume, make your voice a little more breathy until your singing is almost like a whisper.

Here's How You'll Know if Your Fade-Out Is Working. If it's making *you* tired and putting *you* to sleep, then it's going to do the same for your baby. While you're doing your Fade-Out you should start feeling very drowsy.

This gauge works as your baby grows as well. For instance, whenever I go camping with my kids, I make up a bedtime story for them because it's too dark to read from a book. The story always starts out with a simple plotline—maybe it's about a girl who meets a dolphin on the beach and they have a short adventure. But at a certain point, when I feel like my kids are turning a corner and are starting to get sleepy, the story changes and gets really, really *boring*. So boring that it's hard for me to even tell it without falling asleep myself. It often sounds like this:

"Then the girl walked on the beach and looked at all the shells on the sand. She picked up a shell and admired its colors. Then she put it into her bag. She kept walking and saw another shell she loved, so she put that one in her bag. She picked up another shell, and another, and another, and another."

Feeling increasingly sleepy with your baby is exactly the effect you want. It's a good example of co-regulation: you soothe your baby, your baby starts to relax, you notice your baby relaxing so you relax more, and so on. Both of you feeling so relaxed with each other is another reason lullabies are a prime time to connect with your baby.

THE WIND-DOWN

There's another trick that will ensure the success of your lullaby. It's the Wind-Down.

Parents in my classes often describe their bedtime routine—bath, diaper, swaddle, feed, maybe book. Then they sing the lullaby only for a couple minutes before putting the baby to sleep.

Your bedtime routine will be *much* more effective if you start singing (or listening to) the lullaby much earlier than that. Your goal is to give your baby plenty of time to settle down from their day. Here's how that should look:

About an hour before your baby normally goes to bed:

○ Reduce the lights.
○ Turn off phones or any devices that might be making noise.
○ Speak more softly.
○ Move more slowly.
○ Start to sing your lullaby while you take your baby out of the bath.
○ Continue singing while you dress them, feed them, etc.
○ Continue singing while you cradle them for a while before putting them down.

For the first six months you'll be singing your lullaby on repeat for a while. Your Wind-Down should be loooooooong. You want to give your baby plenty of time to associate the lullaby with getting sleepy. But eventually, as your baby gets used to it, you'll only need to sing the first line of the chorus.

"THE TALE OF THE HALF CHORUS"

I remember one night I was putting my one-year-old to sleep in the bedroom and my sister-in-law was sitting on the bed, feeding her newborn. I sang half a line of our lullaby—"Sleep my baby, sleep my baby"—and put her in the crib. She instantly quieted down, rolled over, and went to sleep. My sister-in-law sat with her jaw open. She later asked, "How did you do that so fast?"

The answer was that by that time my baby had completely paired the lullaby with sleep. I had spent months singing it every night, doing a long Wind-Down while singing it and then a Fade-Out as she went down. She was like Pavlov's dogs, who only needed one ring of the bell to know exactly what was going on and to have a physical response to the stimulus.

Common Lullaby FAQs

I'm a terrible singer. Should I not sing a lullaby to my baby?

Remember Chapter 4? Your baby wants to hear *you* over anyone else, including a recording of Beyoncé singing the most beautiful lullaby you can think of. Your voice will be the most soothing and the most emotional regardless of whether you think you can sing well. Your baby thinks you're a rock star.

"I finally got my husband to start singing the lullaby to our baby too. He's insecure about it. He says the baby will be traumatized forever if he sings to him. I told him how it works so well and that he should shut the door and even put on white noise if he needs to. I think he's been experimenting with it. I hope he does it more so he can feel how peaceful bedtime can be." (Alisha, mom of Jaya)

I hope he does too. That baby wants to hear him. And he'll end his day with a smile.

Whenever I start to sing our lullaby, my baby starts to cry. So I guess it doesn't work for my baby?

Your baby is crying because it *is* working. It means that at this point they associate the song with sleep. The lullaby's job is not to make your baby *like* going to sleep, especially if they're newly on the move and want to keep exploring. Rather, it's to help them mentally prepare, trigger a physical response, relax their body, and help them transition. Even if your baby is crying, stick with it. It's a phase.

Can my husband and I each have a different lullaby? I sing one from my culture in a different language.

Yes! Your baby is so smart. They quickly learn to associate your lullaby with you and your partner's with them. As long as you sing one lullaby consistently with your baby, they will develop a response to it.

Should I have a different song for putting my baby to sleep at night and a different song for naps?

Your baby is developing an association to the song and falling asleep. They're not as concerned with how long they will be going to sleep for or whether it's nighttime. You can use the same song anytime you're putting your baby to sleep to reinforce your baby's response to it.

What if my baby becomes more alert when I sing the lullaby?

That's possible. You know by now that there is no one technique that works for all parents and babies. Your baby probably becomes more alert because they sense that you are having a true Bubble Moment. They feel your engagement and are excited to bask in your full attention. That's OK. Give them a minute. Maybe they need a longer Fade-Out or a slower Wind-Down.

Make Bedtime More Enjoyable

The point of this book is not to give you ways to get your baby to have a longer night's sleep. At this point you know that there are many controversial opinions out there about how best to do it. The goal of this book is to give you tools to *enjoy* putting them to sleep more and to build your connection in the process. Your baby will eventually sleep. I promise. So much of parenting is surrendering to the idea that right now your schedule is not how you wish it would be but knowing that this will not last forever.

You might relate to what Cory said one day in class: "The hardest thing for me is feeling like I need to figure out the schedule. What can I do to make it so that she has a good night's sleep so she naps well, etc. I wish I didn't think about that as much. Makes me less present because I'm focusing on that. Using a lullaby with her doesn't solve all of my anxiety, but at least I know we'll have a nice moment before she goes to bed and that she'll probably go down without too much of a fight."

I definitely identify with Cory. When I had my first baby I was obsessed with getting my baby to nap and sleep. That's all I thought about. I'd go out to a class and time the feeding precisely so that he would sleep when we got home and I would have alone time. I needed my own time so badly.

The problem was I was so focused on figuring out his schedule, like an army general, that I wasn't enjoying him as much as I could have been. It took me three babies to finally figure out how to do that.

It was only with my third that I went out to places without worrying about the timing of her naps, knowing that it would end up working out. I tried to stay on schedule, but most of the time I was off. But I *enjoyed* her. I played with her more and was more relaxed when I took her on outings.

Now when I see parents who are able to let the stress of controlling the baby's schedule go and simply enjoy their baby, I smile. I wish I could go back and feel that way with my first two.

Bubble Moment: THE WIND-DOWN

- 💜 Bring down the lights.
- 💜 Turn off devices and noises.
- 💜 Lower the volume of your voice.
- 💜 Speak more slowly.
- 💜 Move more slowly as you hold your baby and get them ready for bed.
- 💜 Start to sing your lullaby way before you are ready to put them down. Sing while you're getting them dressed, feeding, swaddling, etc.
- 💜 Move to Fade-Out.

11

Your Daily Groove

IN THIS CHAPTER, YOU'LL LEARN HOW TO
MAKE YOUR REPEATED EVERYDAY ACTIVITIES
LESS BORING AND MORE BONDING.

It's our sixth class, and as we sing the "Good Morning" song, one of the moms breezes in, cheeks red, hair frazzled, baby in the carrier. She apologizes for being late, and as she recovers from her rush, I think back to when I was a new mom. I laugh to myself about how I dealt with my new mom stress. I needed control like a scuba diver needs an oxygen tank. I wasn't one of those moms who accepted the turmoil of baby care with grace and surrender. I needed order!

Before I went to a class like this, I'd try to time my baby's nap and feeding perfectly so he'd be alert at the meeting and ready to sleep again once we were home. Good plan, right? Of course, it didn't always work out so neatly. And when it didn't, my internal drill sergeant had a fit.

I never cared too much about schedules before having a baby. In fact, I was usually late to everything. Post-baby I became militaristic with time. In T-minus 15 minutes the baby needs to feed. In T-minus 45 minutes we leave for class. No tolerance for error!

Did we keep to our 15-minute increments? Hell no. We'd be on our way out the door, on schedule, when he'd poop and need a diaper change. Again. Or he wouldn't fall asleep in the allotted time, and I'd spend the rest of the day feeling defeated. We'd failed our task, general!

Not the most bonding-conducive environment.

By my third baby I gave up on a schedule strictly governed by time. I had a general idea of when she needed to eat and sleep, and I followed her cues more closely. I didn't obsess over how my day "should" look, and that gave us space to simply *be*. It was liberating, and in the end, we both got more rest together.

You may not need to go through two babies to learn that lesson. Maybe you're more accepting about letting your baby lead you unpredictably through your day. Or maybe, like me, you're grasping for a reliable timetable. Likely, you fall somewhere in between.

Wherever you are on the spectrum of how you're handling this colossal change to your day, this chapter can help. It's not going to give you a set schedule of when your baby should feed and nap down to the minute. You can find schedules like that all over the Internet (but be forewarned—they never work quite that way). Instead, it will provide a framework to help you *enjoy* those routine moments. And, as a bonus, it will help you establish your routine and have a more predictable day.

The Accountable Activities

We've said this already, but it's worth repeating—you can't be present with your baby all the time. It wouldn't even be healthy! To be a good parent, you need to have your own interests, relationships, and self-care.

But there are specific times during your day when you can hold yourself accountable to being fully present with your baby. Why? Because you're with your baby *anyway*.

I'm talking about those activities that feel like Groundhog Day because you do them so often. The repetition can sometimes be boring and grueling. These activities include:

○ Feeding
○ Diaper changing
○ Bathing
○ Putting to sleep

You change your baby's diaper 82 times a week, give or take. You feed and put them to sleep every few hours. These activities are the rote work of parenting. They're the tasks required to care for your baby's basic needs. Good job, parent, for learning how to do them efficiently and keeping up with them day in and day out.

Sometimes you're present with your baby as you do these activities and catch a moment of giggles with them. Other times you're on the phone, watching a show, or going through the motions that have become second nature. That's natural. You do it so often at this point it's like brushing your teeth. You probably don't end your day thinking fondly of your morning brush as a special moment.

But if you're with your baby *anyway* during these tasks and don't have the time or energy to engage meaningfully with your baby for much of the day, why not make these into Bubble Moments? If you manage to do it right, you might not spend your day carrying guilt around, knowing that there's diaper changing around the corner.

How do you do it? **By finding the ritual in the routine.**

From Routine to Ritual

When I use the word *ritual* here, I'm not talking about religious rituals; rather, what we've come to know in modern society as daily rituals. These are actions that you do *intentionally* during your day, often to increase productivity, reduce stress, manage time, or feel more present.[125]

How is ritual different from routine? In *Ritual Theory, Ritual Practice*, Catherine Bell writes: "Ritualization is a matter of various culturally specific strategies for setting some activities off from others." Meaning turning an activity into a ritual has to do with your intention and using specific strategies. Many activities can become rituals; it just depends on your desire to do so.[126]

Why is this worth doing? Because daily rituals have been shown to reduce anxiety, add meaning to the daily grind, and connect people to one another. Sharing a ritual with others increases your social bonding and makes you feel part of a group and a shared experience.[127] Another good reason? It beats the boredom.

The question is: Is there a way to make the grind of parenting easier *and* more enjoyable for you both? Is there a way to go from routine to ritual?

Rituals can reduce anxiety and provide meaning to daily routine.

Yes. One of the best ways in my book is through *music*.

We already talked about how your baby is tuned in to rhythm and music from day one. They remember and respond to songs that were sung to them in utero, and it regulates their heart rate and lowers their cortisol. Music also helps them synchronize with you as we discussed in Chapter 4.

Similarly, music has a huge effect on *your* well-being.[128] It reduces stress, improves cognitive functioning, aids in deeper sleep, improves memory, relieves pain, and increases motivation.

Best of all, when you have musical interactions with your baby, you both feel happier and more connected to each other. One study that compared play interactions between parents and babies with musical interactions made a fascinating discovery: "Musical interactions were found to provide more opportunities for positive emotional arousal and synchronization, which are the basic characteristics of quality interactions and essential for future child development."[129]

Musical interactions elicited more feelings of joy for both parents and babies. They also inspired more synchronization, which leads to bonding.

So how can you make your day more predictable, more manageable, *and* more fun and connected? By incorporating *music*.

Remember the preschool teacher who relies on music to get through the day?[130] They use music for two goals: **transitions and learning.**

We talked about using music for learning language in Chapter 9. Now let's focus on the use of music for transitions. In the classroom, songs help the kids know *when* to move from one activity to the next and *what* to do as they shift.

One study shows that teachers feel that songs are especially crucial for helping the dual language learners in their classes understand what each activity entails.

This is particularly relevant for us because dual language students often don't speak English fluently—just like your baby! For them, songs help because the kids didn't need to rely solely on language but can grow accustomed through a melody they recognize.

Even when the dual language students don't understand specific words, the consistent melody and lyrics help them associate the song with the expected behavior.

Music can make your day more predictable, more manageable, more enriching for your baby, and more enjoyable for you both.

That sounds familiar, right? It's what we talked about in the last chapter when we learned about lullabies. But that hack is not just for bedtime. Songs can help you with each of your routine moments throughout your day. And when used consistently, they can release you from the grind of a timetable but still provide structure.

. . . .

Recap: WHAT MAKES SONGS SO GREAT FOR BABIES?

1. They repeat the same way each time.
2. They're soothing to your baby.
3. They hold your baby's attention.
4. They regulate your baby's breath and mood.

But songs during your daily routine aren't just beneficial for your baby. If used correctly, they can help *you* feel more in control of your day and more connected to your baby.

What Makes Songs Great for *You*?

1. They help you organize your day and keep you focused.
2. They give you a feeling of routine and control.
3. They're a connection booster with your baby.

. . . .

When you use songs during your day, you'll start to see your day as consisting of chunks of time rather than minutes and hours. And by now you know that your baby isn't that great at keeping to a schedule of minutes and hours. Take a break, drill sergeant.

Below we'll talk about your Accountable Activities and how music can help transition in and out of those activities. But first let's remember our end goal—**connection**—and see how music during your day can help you turn your attention away from *minutes* and toward *moments*, away from *time* and toward cute little *toes*.

Adding music to those simple tasks can pull you out of the monotony, add playfulness, and increase your mood. That "Poop Song" you're singing, or "Splish Splash" in the bath, is not just for your baby but even more so for *you*. It keeps you engaged and interested.

Don't say it, *sing* it.

Wait a second. Why can't you just *tell* your baby you're about to change their diaper? Or feed? Or put them down for a nap? You can do that too. But your baby actually prefers to hear you *singing* over speaking.[131] Researchers believe that the reason for that may be that singing holds more emotion than speaking, and babies respond to that.

How to Ritualize with Music

To add oomph to your routine, try pairing a song with each task, similar to the preschool teacher. But wait, are you imagining an infantilizing and annoying preschool teacher? You don't have to be one. This is all about bringing your version of cool to your baby's day.

Let's first focus on your most frequent baby-care tasks, or what I call your Accountable Activities (besides going to sleep, which we covered in the last chapter):

1. Waking up
2. Changing diapers
3. Feeding

Even if you head off to work early, spend the day on calls, or strap the baby on for a day of errands, you're probably still doing at least two of these every day.

Your Morning Ritual

"Going to get Raya from her crib every morning was always my favorite moment of the day, but since I started singing our morning song it got even better. As soon as she hears it she jumps up, so excited. She knows it's our song and giggles as I sing it. Honestly, it's the best thing in the world." (Neha, mom of Raya)

You know how some people naturally wake up in the morning with a smile, and some feel like the morning light is attacking them like a bear in the wild? Well, you have a say in whether your baby will be a morning person or not.

It's true that temperament, genetics, and circumstance play a part. But how we wake up has a lot to do with habit as well, and our behavior is often a reflection of those around us. That's especially true for your baby.

So I'm proposing this: Despite the fact that you had to wake up to your baby 17 times last night, the bottle spilled in the middle of the night, and you haven't showered in three days, greet your baby in the morning with a song.

I know, sometimes it's the *last* thing you want to do. But it's powerful. A morning song is a reset. It can start your day on the right foot no matter what came before it.

"Uh-oh," I can hear you saying: "You think that after a night of wake-ups, before I had coffee, when I'm already fantasizing about a nap and can barely walk straight, I can *sing a song*?"

Yes, I do. Because it will be a bigger energy boost than any cup of coffee can give you.

You're teaching your baby something important that they will take with them for the rest of their lives: It's up to us to start the day out right. Often all it takes is raising the corners of our mouths and greeting the day with a song.

A morning song is a bigger boost of energy than any cup of coffee can provide.

Obviously, sometimes you just can't. You're too overwhelmed, too exhausted, and that's OK. But I'm hoping this will be your nudge to give it a shot and see what happens.

Morning is an opportunity for a reset. You get to emotionally start over. And your sweet baby is eagerly waiting for you like a super fan at a Taylor Swift concert. All they want is for you to come

What Your Morning Song Signals to Your Baby

1. **It's Morning!**

   When you sing your morning song, you're saying to your baby, "It's morning now! It's time to play and be together." It wasn't morning yet when they woke at 3 a.m., and that's why you didn't sing the song. Now it's time to wake up. Eventually your baby will catch on.

2. **We're Together Again!**

   Your morning song comes after a night (fingers crossed!) of sleep and (possibly physical) separation. Singing a song is a way to celebrate your *reunion* and make it that much sweeter. This goes back to the idea of attachment theory. If you're consistent with your morning song, your baby will learn that you always show up. It's a way to start your day with the sweetest Bubble Moment there is.

3. **It's Time to Transition**

   Imagine this: You're waking up slowly in your bed, and someone comes to gently sing you a song as you open your eyes and adjust from your quiet space to the chaos of the world. Sound nice? Your morning song is a way to help your baby ease into the day. Moving from their dark and quiet room and into a space where there's light, noise, and movement can be jarring for your baby. Singing them through this transition helps them make the shift in a gentle way.

to them. You don't even need to sing. But if you do, imagine how ecstatic your little fan will be.

You know how people say, "One day you'll look back on these days and wish you had more of them?" Well that's not exactly true. It's *hard* and you don't wish for more sleepless nights. But here's what I can promise you: If you set your ritual now with your baby, you won't have to yearn for the past. I still sing my morning song to my 8-year-old and 11-year-old. Yeah, the 11-year-old says, "Stop singing!" But I can see a little smile in the corner of his mouth as he does.

Here's what Alicia said about finding her morning song: "I didn't realize it, but we have a morning song. I've always sort of sung 'good morning, good morning' to Connor but thought I was just saying it in a sing-songy way. The other day my mother heard it and she said, "You're singing the song I sang to you when you were a baby! It's from 'Singing in the Rain.'" I realized I'd been singing that same melody without being aware that I remembered it from when I was a girl."

Need some ideas for a morning song? Check out this playlist.

Diaper-Changing Ritual

I bet you didn't realize how deep in poop you'd be as a parent. How many times a day do you deal with it—checking, smelling, cleaning? Add to that a delightful wrestling match if you're baby wants to be on the move.

So what can you do? Whistle while you work. Or rather, sing while you wipe.

A Diaper-Changing Song Is Your Savior.
Here's Why

✴ **It's a Bell**. Ding ding ding! Diaper changing is about to be in progress. All poopy pants on deck. If you start to sing your diaper-changing song as you are bringing the diaper and as you start to undress your baby, then they will know it's coming. Part of what they hate so much is that you are interfering with their exploration. So they protest: "What are you doing? I was just in the middle of something." A song can let them know that diaper changing is on the horizon and can help them prepare.

✴ **It's a Stopwatch**. Within a few times of you singing it while you're changing your baby, they'll start to recognize your song—the middle and the end of it.[132] Often in my groups, babies as young as eight months old start to clap toward the end of the song because they know it's about to end.

You can use your song as a way to tell your baby how long the diaper changing will take. This will give your baby a sense of control over the situation and the knowledge that it won't last forever and they'll be playing again soon.

Don't have a diaper-changing song? Check out this playlist.

But here's an even better idea: Write your own. Actually, you might have already done so without realizing it. Many parents in my groups tell me they sing silly ditties like "Poopy Pants," "Stinky Baby," or my fave: "Don't Pee in My Face." One dad recently told me he sings "She's a very stinky girl" to the tune of Rick James's "Super Freak" ("She's a very freaky girl . . . ").

Maybe you always tend to say something to your baby when you're about to change their diaper. Something like, "Let's go,

poopy pants!" That could turn into your short ditty. (Keep reading for how to write your very own diaper song.)

Feeding Ritual

If you're nursing and your baby isn't eating solids yet, then those
pre-feeding moments might be a cakewalk. You just pull out the
boob and your baby is served an instant meal. But if your baby takes
a bottle or has already started solids, then you know that meal prep
can feel a lot like a tiger waiting for the zookeeper to arrive with
dinner. You don't want to be hanging out in that cage. Your baby
is growing and getting hungrier and hungrier, and that's great.
But along with their rapid development comes the need to eat *now*.

Here's a story: When I was pregnant with my first, I felt nauseous
for a lot of the day, but especially when I was hungry. I realized that
when I'd start to feel hunger coming on I had about 20 minutes
until I'd lose it and need food *now*.

One day, my husband and I were walking through a museum
when my hunger clock started ticking. I told him we didn't have
long to find a place to eat. It took us forever to find the cafeteria,
and by the time we did, I was a wreck. In the café they gave us a pin
to attach to our shirt with a graphic of a fork and spoon. When we
left, we held on to those pins. From then on, every time I started
to get hungry, my husband put the pin on his shirt. It signaled
to us both that we were on a mission to find a
place to eat and had about 15 minutes to do it.
(Weren't those pre-baby moments so charming?
When we could focus only on our own needs?)

Your baby feels a lot like I did in the museum.
Your feeding song is going to act like the pin. It's
a way to tell your baby, "It's OK, I'm on it. Food is
coming soon."

Reasons to Have a "Your Order's Coming Right Up" Song

⭐ **It's a Bell.** In this case the song helps your baby know you are indeed working on their food and not just milling around the kitchen. Once they become accustomed to the song, they'll hear it and know food is on its way.

⭐ **It's a Soother.** The music helps them relax and calm down. It also helps you do the same. Not only that, modeling calming down during what could be a stressful moment for you both teaches your baby how to do it.

⭐ **It's a Timekeeper.** Similar to the diaper-changing song, this song helps your baby understand that they need to wait the length of the song, and they'll have their food by the time you're done singing.

Need a feeding song? Try this playlist.

Other Important Moments to Use a Song

SEPARATION RITUAL

Does your baby cry when you leave the room? Separation anxiety can hit as early as six months and last for a while. Whether you leave them with a nanny, grandma, or your partner, your baby might get distressed when they see you leave. A song can help a lot. Here's why:

It's Connecting. Getting into the habit of singing a song with your baby before you part from them means you're taking a few moments to connect. Otherwise, you may rush through the departure and the separation can feel jarring to your baby.

It's Soothing. Just merely singing (as opposed to saying), "I love you, baby. I'll see you soon!" adds an element of soothing for your baby.

It's a Timekeeper. This time, the timekeeper is for *you*. Leaving your baby when they're crying is not easy. The guilt rushes in! *How can I leave my baby? Look how distressing it is for them!* Having a song with a beginning and end means you won't be sticking around, hoping your baby will come to their senses and realize you'll be back.

Having a song for separation does not mean your baby will immediately stop crying or be OK with you leaving. It is developmentally appropriate for them to feel angry or upset that you're leaving. But the song will help them learn that when you sing it, it means you're leaving but will return.

GETTING DRESSED RITUAL

There are so many pieces of clothing to keep track of and get onto your baby's squirmy body! Endless onesies pulled over their head, billions of tiny socks stranded on sidewalks, snowsuits to stuff your baby into before heading out into the cold.

Dressing your baby is another one of those tasks that happens multiple times daily. And you know what that means—music to the rescue!

This is going to be the song you sing during the entire process of putting all the layers on. You'll keep singing it even through the tears that come with putting one more layer over their head, and here's why:

It's a Bell. Ding ding ding! It's time to get you dressed. You'll start singing the song as you approach with the layers. You're signaling that the dressing won't last forever, and it means you're heading out right after.

It's a Comfort. Singing a song relaxes you both. If it's a song that's fun to sing, then you might even enjoy singing it, and that will help turn the activity into a positive one.

It's a Motivator. Depending on the song you choose, singing a song while you get your baby dressed can be a way to promise you both some fun once you're done—more playing, going outside, going to meet people.

It's a Teacher's Aid. If your song involves listing the clothing parts, it'll help you remember them. *And* it will teach your baby the names of those items because of the repetitive nature of the song.

Need a getting dressed song? There are some ideas in this playlist.

Write Your Own.
It's Not as Crazy as You Think.

You can find some great songs out there. Check the playlists I put together. But the *best* song will be the one *you* write with your baby. Why? Because it's perfectly catered to you both.

After I graduated from college, I wanted to sing in a jazz band. I searched around for musicians and quickly realized that it would be an expensive affair to pay musicians for gigs. I was often only paid in meals. So I decided I'd need to learn how to play the guitar myself.

I took some lessons and realized, *Uh-oh. These jazz songs are really hard to play.* That's when I decided to write my own songs. I could use the chords I knew and could even limit the melodies to my vocal range. I'm no Ella Fitzgerald.

What I realized was that writing songs was much more fun and gratifying for me than playing other people's. I could sing anything that flowed through my quirky mind. In fact, my first song started like this:

I've got a problem
I can't write songs like Elvis Costello
Because he suffers too much
And I don't.

Parents, your baby wants to hear *your* quirky song that no one else but you could have come up with. It will sound best when you're singing it because it will be tailored to your voice, inflection, and rhythm.

And then years from now, when your kid is talking to friends, he's going to say, "My mom used to sing this silly song to me that she made up. I'll always remember it." Don't be surprised if they go on to sing it to their baby.

That Sounds Great, but I Can't Write a Song!

I know. Most people don't spend their time writing songs. But hear me out—you are already a mere step away.

Here's what I mean. When you speak to your baby, you use what psychologists call Motherese or Parentese. That's the sing-songy, exaggerated tone you reserve only for your baby. Do you know what I mean? Think of how you might say "hiiiiiii" to your baby. Try it out loud right now. Did you notice the melody in your intonation? It usually happens in a bell curve. Your voice starts low, you slide up to quite a high tone, and then you come down again.

Similarly, when your baby is upset, you descend with your voice. Think of how you might say, "It's OK," or "Come here, baby." Did you notice that your tone dropped toward the end?

You speak that way to your baby because they prefer it and it holds their attention.[133] Not only that, it helps them develop communication skills and regulates their arousal level.[134] The reason your baby responds so well to your Parentese is that you constantly alter it based on your baby's mood, state of arousal, and attention.

You don't do this with adults. I bet that when your partner walks in the door you don't use that same sing-songy tone to say, "Hiiiii. How was your day?" That would feel pretty strange for everyone.

So what does Parentese have to do with writing a song? You're already melodic. All you need to do is go with it.

Here's what I mean. The next time you're about to change your baby's diaper, notice what you say to your baby. You might say something like, "Time to change your diaper!" Now imagine you're saying it to your baby. Try to mimic exactly how you'd say it.

Do you notice how you say the word *diaper*? Do you rise with the "di" and descend with the "per"? Or does your voice go up high with the "per"?

To turn the way you speak to your baby into a song, all you need to do is repeat that sentence a few times *exactly the way you'd say it to your baby*. It might not sound like a song at first, but repeating your sing-songy communication with your baby, even if it's just one line, is practically half of your song. Then all you need to do is add one more line.

Maybe it could be something with your baby's name or a silly term you use when you're changing their diaper, like poopy pants or stinky. So it might sound like this:

Let's go change your diaper
Let's go change your diaper
Zaya's going to be so clean, so clean.

In class parents are always surprised at how fast we're able to write a song together. Using the way they naturally speak to their baby, it takes less than five minutes! They're even more surprised at how catchy the song ends up being.

You don't need Stevie Wonder to write your song. Just use the lyrics and melody you're *already* doing. That's it!

Another option is to use a melody that exists and change the lyrics a bit. For instance, to the tune of "This Is the Way We Wash Our Hands," try "This is how we put on our pants, put on our pants, put on our pants."

Tips for Going from Routine to Ritual

1. **Make a decision to make the mundane moments more special.** You're doing them anyway; they might as well be enjoyable for you both.
2. **Leave the phone in the other room when you pick them up in the morning,** change them, get them dressed.
3. **Come up with songs you'll use for the Big Three routine moments:** sleep, feed, diaper change.
4. **Notice what you say to your baby before and while you do these tasks with them.** Try to repeat what you said with the same inflection to start your own song.
5. **Use sensations to stay present.** Notice how your baby feels; the touch of their skin; the way they smell, sound, taste. Focus on the way your body feels as you are doing these activities.

> **Bubble Moment: MORNING SONG**
>
> 💙 Take a breath as you approach your baby in the morning. Shed the frustrations of the night before with your exhale.
>
> 💙 Sing your morning song softly to your baby as you approach.
>
> 💙 Pick up your baby and continue to sing in the dark and quiet room they were sleeping in.
>
> 💙 Continue singing as you walk out to the light and chaos of the living space.
>
> 💙 Let your baby take their time adjusting to the light and to being awake.

But I Can't Sing!

Parent, I know this may not be an easy ask. And even though we talked about ways to overcome vocal insecurities in Chapter 4, you may still feel very hesitant to let your inner Mariah bust out while changing a diaper. That's OK. I get it.

Remember, even though I'm a musician and music therapist, I didn't sing immediately with my first baby. The parents in my classes often have a Mary Poppins image of me prancing around the house, singing "A Spoonful of Sugar" as I care for my calm baby.

Nope. When I had my first baby, I didn't sing a note. It took me a while to unleash my inner music with my baby. So, if you haven't found it yet, I know how you feel and so do many other parents.

Here are some tips for turning your time with your baby into your very own quirky, loving, silly, and playful musical.

HOW TO FIND YOUR OWN SOUND OF MUSIC

Give It Time. It was pointless for me to berate myself when my own inner music was MIA. I needed to give myself time to feel comfortable enough to access it. Be patient. It will come. If you read this chapter and were intrigued by the use of songs to ease your day, then songs will come to you. I promise.

Music with Emotion. Usually, the music you heard when you were younger—whether in college, high school, grade school, or younger—holds emotion within it. Use those songs to make your ritual more meaningful for you both.

No Need to Belt. You're not taking the act on the road, so start small. Try humming softly to your baby. Maybe it's a lullaby, a song you love, or a song you're making up. No one else needs to hear.

Notice the Magic. When my daughter was about 10 months old, I found that every time I would sing to her she immediately started to sing along. She wasn't singing the lyrics or the melody exactly, but she was definitely singing along. Notice how your baby reacts when you sing your daily songs. Do they smile? Perk up? Join along? Look into your eyes?

Sing for Your Fan. We all have an insecure part of ourselves that has listened to judgments from the past. Those are the voices that make our body tense up the moment we start to sing, especially in our throat. But now you've got a different audience who loves your voice unconditionally. Take a moment to appreciate your adoring judge. It might just make you take in deeper breaths and sing from your belly, not your throat.

Channel Your Inner Julie Andrews. If you're starting to feel comfortable with it, experiment with turning your routine moments into a mini musical. Go big! Skip to get a diaper while singing with a sly smile. Throw up the diaper cream and catch it in your hand. Find the free and playful part of yourself that brings lightness to everyday tasks.

Find Your Classes. I'm biased here, but I've seen how a class can transform parents from mostly silent at home with their baby to supercalifragilistic. A good class can inspire you to take some vocal risks, free your inner songwriter, and unleash your rhythm master.

Involve Everyone. Is your partner shy with their voice? Once you feel a bit more comfortable with yours, share your routine songs with your partner. Let them feel how powerful they can be as well. This is a win-win for all—your baby will have more opportunities to develop associations with your songs and you'll be infusing your home with more playfulness.

You have inner music. We all do. Once you experiment with this a bit, you might be surprised at how easily your songs flow.

Your Magic Wands

IN THIS CHAPTER, YOU'LL LEARN THREE
TECHNIQUES FOR GETTING THROUGH
THE WITCHING HOUR.

I arrive to class frazzled today. I realized my bike had a flat tire halfway there and had to get it home and catch a cab to class. I'm sweating and feeling terrible about arriving late. I know what a feat it is for the parents to get to class with their babies.

We do our opening songs, our Three Breaths exercise, and the "Bikeride" song to get the babies moving. But even after all that I'm still not feeling settled. I take a breath and start to play a song that I know always grounds me. It's "Peace Like a River."

I first heard it when I was working as a music leader in a school. Its simple, predictable melody and spiritual but not religious lyrics immediately calmed me when I heard it.

For years after I forgot about it until I had my first baby. Then I heard Elizabeth Mitchell's beautiful rendition, and when I did, I instantly felt peaceful once again. I started singing it with my baby and in classes whenever I needed to soothe myself. It became my go-to when I needed grounding to be effective as a group leader. It slowed me down and prompted me to take deeper breaths and sing in a more resonant way. And because I did, the group shifted, too, and relaxed along with me.

In this chapter we're going to cover three effective strategies to get you through your toughest moments. Think of them as your magic wands for the witching hour, or when your day starts to feel loooooooong, you know you still have hours to go, your baby is fussy, you're exhausted, and you wonder how you're going to make it until bedtime.

1. Your Grounding Song

Remember Mary Poppins's bag? It was magical. It held so much more than was physically possible—a hatstand, a lamp, a mirror, a plant. You know what else is like that? Yup—music.

To explain what I mean I have to tell you about the first time I got my heart broken. I'm in third grade, sitting on a swing during recess. Next to me, on another swing, is my friend Sheila. The boy I have a crush on, Danny, walks over to Sheila, stands over her, and says, "If you stand up, I'll kiss you." My heart drops. He likes her and not me! I'm shattered. On the bus ride home, I'm in a daze. There's a song playing on the radio. It's "Total Eclipse of the Heart." I sit in a trance, listening to the song and feeling it so deeply, as if it was written for me. Who says nine-year-olds don't understand heartbreak?

Every moment from then on, when I heard that song, it all came rushing back—the heartbreak, the rejection, the yearning, the insecurity, and also the nostalgia, the empathy for my young self, the naivete. When I hear that song I can almost feel the chains of the swing in my hands. It's like Mary Poppins's bag. The song holds within it many sensations and memories that come tumbling out with a listen.

Do you have a song like that? One that touched you at a pivotal moment in your life and now brings back all the feelings of that time? Maybe you have many. Songs are like buttons that can release emotions that live deep within our body. That's because the autobiographical memory network and music are integrated in a similar region of the brain (the medial prefrontal cortex).[135] Music triggers memories and sensations from our past.

Years from now you may hear a song you've been listening to lately or singing to your baby and immediately have the feels—the extreme love, the joy, the frustration, the exhaustion that you feel now. When I hear my baby's morning song now, I swear I can almost feel my milk coming in.

How can you use this information? By finding your **grounding song.**

A grounding song is a way for you to put a loving hand on your own shoulder and say to yourself, *It's OK. You're OK.* The best part is that it works on you and your baby at the same time.

Your grounding song helps you regulate your breathing and calm your nervous system.

What is your grounding song? Is there a song in your life that triggers a relaxing response from your nervous system? Does it make you take deeper breaths and move a bit slower?

How to Establish Your Grounding Song

1. **Song.** Choose a song that makes you breathe slower, take deeper breaths, sense warmth in your chest, and feel heavier in your seat.
2. **Sing.** Sing or play your song when you're feeling particularly stressed (related to your baby's fussing or not).
3. **Slow.** Move slowly as you sing, even if your baby continues to fuss; let the song work its magic on you.
4. **Repeat.** Continue using your song during difficult moments.

SHARING YOUR GROUNDING SONG

When you sing your grounding song, your baby will absorb the impact that your song has on you and will mirror your transformation. And then one day your grounding song may even turn into their grounding song.

Here's how I know. Years after I started using "Peace Like a River" as my grounding song, something happened in one of my classes.

One of the moms shared upsetting news she had gotten at her baby's medical appointment. She found out that the baby had a chronic condition that could affect him throughout his life. The mom shared the news quickly. She said she wanted everyone to know but didn't want to take up too much time in the group. She was visibly shaken.

We all sat with the news for a moment, and some members near her reached out and touched her back or knee. And then they looked to me to tell them—where do we go from here?

I felt overwhelmed. I was distressed by the news of this mama and baby whom I'd grown to know and love. She had come to my class with her first baby as well, and at this point we were friends.

The feeling in the room was heavy. The parents were probably flooded with feelings— wondering if their baby was OK, thankful they weren't in the same situation and feeling guilty for that thought, wanting to help the mom feel better but not knowing how. They needed me to lead them somewhere safe and comforting.

I took a deep breath and asked the mom if there was a song she felt like singing. Without being explicit, I was asking what her grounding song was. I hoped that music could provide us with a nonverbal way of supporting her while also allowing us to channel our deeper feelings into the song

The mom said, "Let's sing 'Peace Like a River.'"

I smiled. Of course. Through our years

together in class, my grounding song had become her grounding song. And maybe her grounding song will become her baby's.

As we sang, we were all a bit tearful. The song unleashed lots of feelings at once—concern, sadness, anger, love, fear, hope. We finished and sat quietly, taking deep breaths. It felt as if we were breathing together. That's how it will feel with your baby too.

Bubble Moment: GROUNDING SONG

💜 Think of a song that makes you feel calm, makes you move more slowly, and feels comfortable to sing or play on speakers.

💜 When you're feeling stressed, put on or sing your song.

💜 You can hold your baby as you sing so they'll feel you calm down (and may even calm you back).

💜 Take deep breaths as you sing or listen; sway with the music.

💜 Repeat during difficult moments.

---

2. The Great Outdoors

I had my first baby during winter. Darkness fell around 5 p.m. and so did my spirits. I started noticing that I was watching the front door like a hawk, willing my partner to come home. I had never done that before having a baby, and when I realized I had turned into a housewife from the 1950s, I was mortified. Where was the independent, creative, self-motivated, resourceful woman I once was? What had become of me?

In my lowest moments I found a simple fix that shifted everything: **going outside.**

You might not feel like it. Bundling up your baby demands way more energy than you may have in your "end of the rope" moments, and you may have nowhere to go. But it will do wonders for you both.

For you, walking outside can reduce depression, blood pressure, and chronic pain, and improve cognitive function and cardiovascular functioning.[136],[137],[138] For your baby, going outside can improve their physical and cognitive development and their immune system.[139],[140] Most importantly, it will be a change in scenery and will broaden your view past the walls inside your home.

But here's the best reason to take your baby for a walk outside. Research shows that it will improve their sleep and yours.[141],[142] You can't find a better reason than that right about now.

You don't need to have a destination. The walk itself is the activity, even if it's just for 10 minutes around the block.

3. Dance Party!

You know what else we do in class when the mood is heavy? It shifts the mood every time—we dance! Sure, it's for the babies to feel rhythm, movement, and in sync with their parents, but mostly it's for the parents.

I probably don't have to tell you how beneficial dancing is; you know it from experience. But science backs it up—it improves your mood, reduces stress, and releases serotonin, which makes you feel happier.[143] On top of that, it's a connection booster. In Chapter 4 we talked about how moving to the beat is ingrained in us. We feel more in sync with each other, and our baby, when we do.

In the roughest witching hour moments, when the *last* thing you want to do is get up and dance, when you're so tired you can barely make a bottle for your baby, try it anyway. Put on a Justin Timberlake or Rihanna song and start by standing while holding your baby. Even just a minute of moving to the music can fuel you for the next couple hours.

Find a song that you love dancing to. It doesn't matter how embarrassing it is, how old it is, or how uncool it is. It just has to be a song that gets you excited to move. You can even prepare for your evening crash now by thinking about a few songs that might inspire you to move and putting them in a playlist.

When the sun starts to set, scoop your baby up, put that song on, and go to town. Put all the tasks aside and just let your body move to the beat.

Why Exactly Will Dancing Cure Our Woes?

1. **Music Is an Endorphin.** It actually makes us happy. I know that you've experienced this in the past, so I don't need to elaborate.

2. **Moving to the Beat Gets Us Out of Our Heads and into Our Body.** And that gets us into the present moment. It alleviates spiraling into that go-to internal dialogue: "This sucks." "I'm tired." "Who am I?" "Where is he?" "What do I do?" "I'm *so* tired."

3. **Dancing Is a Workout.** As you know, moving our body even a little bit strenuously energizes us in the long run. It reduces stress and releases endorphins and physical tension.

4. **Dancing with Our Baby Brings Us in Sync with Each Other.** Babies love to dance and move to a rhythm. In fact, they do it on their own from a very early age. When we move them with us to the rhythm of the music, we are syncing our breathing and our mood, all while holding them close. It's the closest simulation of the womb.

5. **A Dance Party Is Like a Reset to Your Evening.** Try it. You'll see that that mood you were feeling a minute ago dissipates into nothing. You might even feel a moment of celebration. You've got a lot to celebrate: You got through the day!

6. **Need a baby-friendly dance party playlist?** Try this one.

Bubble Moment: DANCE PARTY

💜 Put together a playlist of your favorite dance songs so it will be ready when you need it.

💜 Share your playlist with friends and ask them about their favorite dance songs.

💜 Put on a song, pick up your baby, and dance!

💜 If you get tired, put your baby down and dance around them.

💜 Go crazy—no one else sees but your baby.

AFTERWORD:
OUR BUBBLE MOMENT

It's our final class of the series, and the caregivers greet each other with warm hugs as they enter. They've become like family and have supported each other through one of the most monumental periods of their lives. We go around, and each says how the class has impacted them.

Shari says, "This group changed my life as a mom. I look back at how I felt in those first weeks—I was a mess! I'd cry on my way to class because I didn't get the baby ready on time, or when I couldn't get the baby down for a nap. Now I feel like I have a group of friends who have my back. I also feel much more confident as a mom. Well, maybe confident is a strong word. But I feel like I know what I'm doing a little more. We'll see what happens now that Izzy is on the move."

Dear parent, we've had our own sort of Bubble Moment together through this book. I've imagined you reading it while I write, and perhaps you've imagined me speaking to you (and the group) as you read.

At the end of every session we do two things: We look back and we look ahead. Let's do that together here.

First, I wonder what you'll take away from this book. What tip will stick with you as you sit with your baby? Is there one that helps you have a better day or night?

And along with that, what felt challenging and even annoying to hear? Those are important to reflect on as well (and I hope you'll write to me and let me know).

Here are some takeaways parents have shared over the years after taking the class. Maybe you'll find yourself in something that these parents said.

Forget the To-Do List. "This class helped me in so many ways. But one thing in particular was that it helped remind me to be in the moment more. Forget about the to-do list, the piles of laundry, and the dishes in the sink. Just focus on playing and singing to my baby."

Your Baby Just Wants You to Sing. "In the first few months with my baby I felt like I didn't quite know how to communicate with him. My husband was able to turn everything into a jingle and I felt like I needed to do that if I was going to get through to him, but it scared me. I felt like I couldn't sing well enough and was scared my baby would judge me. During the class I realized I needed to just start singing and that everything would be OK. Our lives became much more fun."

Make Bedtime a Bubble Moment. "Bedtime for Otis was the time of day I didn't look forward to. I wasn't sure what would work and if he would go down easily. I also felt very task-oriented and wasn't really connecting with him during the process. After taking this class I have a completely different experience with bedtime. It is actually the time I most look forward to now. We sing a lullaby I love and he seems to love too."

Play Can Be Relaxing. "My favorite moment was the day that Vered asked us to lie on the floor next to our babies and see the world through their eyes. Vered played a quiet tune, and I felt so close to my little guy. And so peaceful. For someone who is constantly planning and strategizing and thinking and worrying—this was a gift beyond measure. Now when I find myself overwhelmed or I realize I've been glued to my phone for too many hours, I lower myself to my baby's level and I try to see what he's seeing."

Bubble Moments Need to Be Enjoyable for You Too. "I enjoy life so much more when my house is clean, but when I spend time with my baby my house gets dirtier and dirtier. So one day I decided to do something for myself and make my bed every day. I had one hand pulling on the sheets and blankets, and the other holding my baby. It took longer and was more work for me, but after a while it became a special time for the two of us. I would play one of my favorite songs and sing and dance around the bed as I made it. It helped me feel like myself again and was my small step toward confidence in my ability to be a mother."

Bubble Moments Get You through the Tough Moments. "I've been doing his noises—saying 'ahhhh' back to him. He stares at me and his eyes get big and he does it back. It feels so good when that happens. It's like we're talking to each other, like we're finally communicating. At night he gets so upset, and I don't know what's wrong. When that happens I think about the happy moments we have when we talk together."

What are some Bubble Moments you've had lately? I hope that when you meet up with your parent friends, you make sure to mention not only the tough moments, of which we know there are many, but also the wonderful moments.

In class each parent says a wonderful and challenging moment they had with their baby during the past week. Sometimes parents struggle to think about the wonderful moments, and the challenging ones cast a dark shadow on the week. But usually at some point there's a shift, and suddenly it's easier to recall the wonderful moments, and it's the challenging ones that don't come to mind. That's always cause for celebration.

Of course, there's always a mix of both challenging and wonderful. But our goal with Bubble Moments is to have enough of the positive ones to paint the others with a lighter shade.

Now let's look at the months ahead with your baby.

What Do I Do with My Baby *Now*?!

At this point maybe your baby is already scooching, crawling, scaling the couch, or even walking. They're learning how to move on their own, with less support from you, and are seeking more independence.

Will all the Bubble Moments we've talked about change? Yes and no. Until now, many of your Bubble Moments happened when your baby was immobile, when it was your job to approach and seek eye contact.

But now that your baby is on the move, a meeting of the gaze is more challenging. Your baby doesn't want to stare into your eyes anymore! They're like sailors on an expedition to find new land. They want to explore, touch, open, close, pull, turn, throw, and smush anything they find.

So what's your job in all this? It's actually *huge*. You're the Motunui to Moana's quest. You're the origin island to their voyage. You're the home base to their home run. Your baby feels emboldened to venture into new territory, knowing that you're waiting for them when they need to rest or recharge.

Margaret Mahler was an Austrian pediatrician and psycho-analyst who coined the term "separation-individuation." Mahler explained that, from around 10 months, infants enter a more autonomous phase. This phase begins with the infant's increased mobility, which allows them to venture out, but they always check back with the caregiver to emotionally refuel. After a few months of being mobile, the infant develops a growing awareness of their separateness from their caregiver, which is empowering but can be scary too.

My son was about 11 months old when I first learned about Mahler's theory and her concept of rapprochement—the push and pull of the baby both wanting to be independent as well as need-ing physical and emotional support from the parent. I remember sitting with my baby on the rug while he tried to pull himself up to standing by holding my knees. When I moved to help him stand, he'd swat my hands away. He wanted to do it on his own, god-dammit, even if it meant falling. He was the perfect case study for Mahler's theory.

As I watched him, a phrase popped into my head: *Mama leave me be, but don't leave me.*

Eventually, it became the chorus of a song. The first verse went like this:

My baby stands up on his two feet
In between my knees holding tight onto me.
And he says Mama help me, but don't hold me up.
I can perfectly handle all that I want, so
Mama leave me be, but don't leave me.

Later I played it for a friend who had a baby the same age. I was surprised that she got tearful as she listened. She said she didn't realize she was feeling so emotional about her baby growing and doing things on his own. She felt like he was a step away from going off to college with no more than a "See ya!" At the same time, she celebrated his growth and appreciated that he wasn't constantly on her physically. She also gained her own independence.

She inspired me to write the final lines:

Baby leave me be, but don't leave me.

Your baby isn't the only one going through an individuation process right now. *You* are. The transition from when your baby is available to be held and cuddled all the time, needing you to do everything for them, to now, when they want their own space and want to learn how to do things on their own, is huge. There's much to mourn.

But there's also celebration! You have your body back, your space back, and your baby is boldly taking the world by storm.

As you continue to grow as a parent while your baby grows beside you, I hope you'll remember to stop a few times a day and have a Bubble Moment with them. It doesn't have to take more than two minutes.

I find that, out of all the things my babies have taught me, the biggest is changing my concept of *time*. They've shown me that "baby time" is slow and have invited me to join them. But they've also sprouted so quickly in front of my eyes, changing and surprising me every day. At this point, time for me is like sitting on a speeding train. The fleeting landscape outside my window is like my kids' rapid growth. But Bubble Moments are what happens inside the train, where everything is still for that moment.

I'll leave you with one last song. I cried as I wrote it. That's always my gauge as to whether someone else will cry as they hear it. And indeed, I can always find the teary-eyed parent staring back at me as I sing:

One day I'll look back
On my afternoons with you,
And I'll say when my baby was too young to move,
I'd play the guitar and he'd gaze into my eyes.
Those were the first days of our lives.
Those were some good days of our lives.

ACKNOWLEDGMENTS

First and foremost, thank you Tsuri. I'm always coming up with new projects to throw myself into, and you are forever encouraging me, never doubting whether my projects are feasible or worthwhile. You support me fully and I feel so lucky to have you as my home base, my friend, my co-parent, and my partner in life.

Thank you Peleg, Lavie, and Alona. You changed me so much that I built a career around understanding what happened. You are each so unique and taught me vastly different ways to be your mama. Peleg, I had my first Bubble Moments with you. You cracked open my heart and out came my first songs about you and us. Lavie, at three months you were in my very first class flashing your irresistible smile. I wrote some of my favorite songs with you and was inspired to keep building Baby in Tune. Alona, with you I finally got it. I understood what it meant to be a wholehearted mother. I leaned in and you reciprocated, always ready to sing along with me.

Thanks Mom, for passing down your love of psychology, handing me Freud and teaching me how to analyze dreams at thirteen.

You were my first reader for this book, and your cheerleading encouraged me to keep going when I doubted myself. I love having you as my mom, my supporter, my friend, and the energetic and loving grandma that you are to my children.

Thanks Dad, for instilling in me the belief that I can do anything, even write a book. It didn't seem so farfetched because I had seen the ones you wrote from an early age. I remember telling you about my idea for this book at that restaurant on the beach. You listened intently as you always do, and said, "Yes. You should absolutely write it." Thank you for pushing me to open doors and follow my curiosity. I appreciate how proud you are of me.

Thank you Benzi, for our many conversations in which you helped me stay on track professionally. You encouraged me to collect the experience I've gathered for the last fifteen years and put it into this book.

Thanks Noa, for our conversations when I was just dipping my toe into the idea of this book. Thank you Cheli, for kickstarting my writing by patiently helping me tease out my thoughts and start to shape them.

Thank you Arietta, for introducing me to attachment theory and being a mentor along the way. I value your work and your warm support greatly.

Thank you Tovah, Tina, Bethany, Paige, and Neha, for being my early readers. Your endorsement means so much to me and gave me energy to put this out into the world.

Thank you to the team who helped turn this book into a reality. Thank you Rea, for helping me put a proposal together, keeping me on task, and introducing me to Rachel. Thank you to my agent, Rachel. I am so grateful that this book resonated with you the way it did. I love having you on my team and am grateful for your willingness to go to bat for me.

Thank you Ann, for believing in this book and in me, and for giving me so much freedom. I enjoyed this process because I felt the faith you had in me to create something great. Thank you Pete, for creating my dream cover; it was exactly what I was hoping for. Thank you Sarah, for your work on the cover, and for being patient and flexible with all of my opinions. Thanks to Chris, for the perfect book design. Thank you Maya, for keeping me on track and moving this project along. Thank you Devorah, and the rest of the team at Countryman Press, for getting this book into the hands of new parents.

Last and most important, thank you to all the parents and babies who have been part of the Tuniverse. You've made this work that I enjoy doing so much possible. You come to classes, sing with me, laugh with me, and, most of all, share authentically in our groups. You've taught me so much about parenting and have made my work meaningful, fun, and gratifying. Thank you for being the ears to my music and eyes to my words. This book is for you.

NOTES

1. Bowlby, John. 1969. *Attachment and Loss.* 2nd ed. Vol. 1. New York: Basic Books.
2. Ainsworth, Mary, Mary Blehar, Everett Waters, and Sally N. Wall. 1978. *Patterns of Attachment: A Psychological Study of the Strange Situation.* New York: Routledge. https://mindsplain.com/wp-content/uploads/2021/01/Ainsworth-Patterns-of-Attachment.pdf.
3. Stern, Daniel N. 1971. "A Micro-Analysis of Mother-Infant Interaction." *Journal of the American Academy of Child Psychiatry* 10, no. 3 (July): 501–17. https://doi.org/10.1016/s0002-7138(09)61752-0. Beebe, Beatrice, and Miriam Steele. "How Does Microanalysis of Mother–Infant Communication Inform Maternal Sensitivity and Infant Attachment?" 2013.*Attachment & Human Development* 15, no. 5–6 (November): 583–602. https://doi.org/10.1080/14616734.2013.841050.
4. Winnicott, D. W. 1971. *Playing and Reality.* Taylor & Francis Ltd.
5. ScienceDaily. 2014. "Four in 10 Infants Lack Strong Parental Attachments." Press release, March 27, 2014. https://www.sciencedaily.com/releases/2014/03/140327123540.htm.
6. Saltman, Bethany. 2020. *Strange Situation: A Mother's Journey into the Science of Attachment.* New York: Ballantine Books.
7. Wong, Y. Joel, Jesse Owen, Nicole T. Gabana, Joshua W. Brown, Sydney McInnis, Paul Toth, and Lynn Gilman. 2018. "Does Gratitude Writing Improve the Mental Health of Psychotherapy Clients? Evidence from a Randomized Controlled Trial." *Psychotherapy Research* 28, no. 2: 192–202. https://doi.org/10.1080/10503307.2016.1169332.
8. Burgoon, Judee K., Laura K. Guerrero, and Kory Floyd. 2016. *Nonverbal Communication.* London: Routledge, Taylor & Francis Group.

9. Krumhuber, Eva, Antony S. R. Manstead, Darren Cosker, Dave Marshall, Paul L. Rosin, and Arvid Kappas. 2007. "Facial Dynamics as Indicators of Trustworthiness and Cooperative Behavior." *Emotion* 7, no. 4: 730–35. https://doi.org/10.1037/1528-3542.7.4.730.

10. Tedder, Janice Lee. 2008. "Give Them *the HUG*: An Innovative Approach to Helping Parents Understand the Language of Their Newborn." *Journal of Perinatal Education* 17, no. 2: 14–20. https://doi.org/10.1624/105812408x298345.

11. Kang, Sun-Mee. 2012. "Individual Differences in Recognizing Spontaneous Emotional Expressions: Their Implications for Positive Interpersonal Relationships." *Psychology* 3, no. 12A: 1183–88. https://doi.org/10.4236/psych.2012.312a175.

12. Slade, Arietta. 2005. "Parental Reflective Functioning: An Introduction." *Attachment & Human Development* 7, no. 3: 269–81. https://doi.org/10.1080/14616730500245906.

13. Fonagy, Peter, Howard Steele, George S. Moran, Miriam Steele, and Anna C. Higgitt. 1991. "The Capacity for Understanding Mental States the Reflective Self in Parent and Child and Its Significance for Security of Attachment." *Infant Mental Health Journal* 13 (Fall): 200–217. https://doi.org/10.1002/1097-0355(199123)12:3<201::AID-IMHJ2280120307>3.0.CO;2-7.

14. Rutherford, Helena J. V., Angela N. Maupin, Nicole Landi, Marc N. Potenza, and Linda C. Mayes. 2016. "Parental Reflective Functioning and the Neural Correlates of Processing Infant Affective Cues." *Social Neuroscience* 12, no. 5: 519–29. https://doi.org/10.1080/17470919.2016.1193559.

15. Leyton, Fanny, Marcia Olhaberry, Rubén Alvarado, Graciela Rojas, Luis Alberto Dueñas, George Downing, and Howard Steele. 2019. "Video Feedback Intervention to Enhance Parental Reflective Functioning in Primary Caregivers of Inpatient Psychiatric Children: Protocol for a Randomized Feasibility Trial." *Trials* 20, no. 1: 268. https://doi.org/10.1186/s13063-019-3310-y.

16. Cassidy, Jude. 2008. "Emotion Regulation: Influences of Attachment Relationships." *Monographs of the Society for Research in Child Development* 59, no. 2–3: 228–49. https://doi.org/10.1111/j.1540-5834.1994.tb01287.x.

17. Brazelton, T. Berry, and J. Kevin Nugent. 2011. *The Neonatal Behavioral Assessment Scale.* London: Mac Keith Press.

18. Stein, Alan, Adriane Arteche, Annukka Lehtonen, Michelle Craske, Allison Harvey, Nicholas Counsell, and Lynne Murray. 2010. "Interpretation of Infant Facial Expression in the Context of Maternal Postnatal Depression." *Infant Behavior and Development* 33, no. 3: 273–78. https://doi.org/10.1016/j.infbeh.2010.03.002.

19. Amankwaa, Linda C., Rita H. Pickler, and Junyanee Boonmee. 2007. "Maternal Responsiveness in Mothers of Preterm Infants." *Newborn and Infant Nursing Reviews* 7, no. 1: 25–30. https://doi.org/10.1053/j.nainr.2006.12.001.

20. Brown, Brené. 2022. "Creating Space." Brené Brown. May 9, 2022. https://brenebrown.com/articles/2022/05/09/creating-space/.

21. Hardin, Jillian S., Nancy Aaron Jones, Krystal D. Mize, and Melannie Platt. 2020. "Parent-Training with Kangaroo Care Impacts Infant Neurophysiological Development & Mother-Infant Neuroendocrine Activity." *Infant Behavior and Development* 58 (February): 101416. https://doi.org/10.1016/j.infbeh.2019.101416.

22. Van Leeuwen, Peter, D. Geue, Marco Thiel, Dirk Cysarz, Silke Lange, Maria Carmen Romano, Niels Wessel, Juergen Kurths, and Dietrich Groenmeyer. 2009.

"Influence of Paced Maternal Breathing on Fetal–Maternal Heart Rate Coordination." *Proceedings of the National Academy of Sciences* 106, no. 33: 13661–66. https://doi.org/10.1073/pnas.0901049106.

23. DeCasper, Anthony J., and Phyllis Prescott. 2009. "Lateralized Processes Constrain Auditory Reinforcement in Human Newborns." *Hearing Research* 255, no. 1–2: 135–41. https://doi.org/10.1016/j.heares.2009.06.012.

24. Smith, Corinne R., and Alfred Steinschneider. 1975. "Differential Effects of Prenatal Rhythmic Stimulation on Neonatal Arousal States." *Child Development* 46, no. 2: 574–78. https://pubmed.ncbi.nlm.nih.gov/1183276/.

25. Trainor, Laurel J. 2007. "Do Preferred Beat Rate and Entrainment to the Beat Have a Common Origin in Movement?" *Empirical Musicology Review* 2, no. 1: 17–20. https://trainorlab.mcmaster.ca/publications/TrainorLJ2007.

26. Iwanaga, Makoto. 1995. "Relationship between Heart Rate and Preference for Tempo of Music." *Perceptual and Motor Skills* 81, no. 2: 435–40. https://doi.org/10.1177/003151259508100215.

27. Teie, David. 2016. "A Comparative Analysis of the Universal Elements of Music and the Fetal Environment." *Frontiers in Psychology* 7 (August): 1158. https://doi.org/10.3389/fpsyg.2016.01158.

28. Groswasser, J., M. Sottiaux, E. Rebuffat, T. Simon, M. Vandeweyer, I. Kelmanson, D. Blum, and A. Kahn. 1995. "Reduction in Obstructive Breathing Events during Body Rocking: A Controlled Polygraphic Study in Preterm and Full-Term Infants." *Pediatrics* 96 (1 Pt 1): 64–68. https://doi.org/ https://doi.org/10.1542/peds.96.1.64.

29. Sammon, M. P., and Robert A. Darnall. 1994. "Entrainment of Respiration to Rocking in Premature Infants: Coherence Analysis." *Journal of Applied Physiology* 77, no. 3: 1548–54. https://doi.org/10.1152/jappl.1994.77.3.1548.

30. RIKEN. 2013. "Why Do Babies Calm Down When They Are Carried?" Press release, April 19, 2013. https://www.riken.jp/en/news_pubs/research_news/pr/2013/20130419_2/.

31. Ohmura, Nami, Lana Okuma, Anna Truzzi, Kazutaka Shinozuka, Atsuko Saito, Susumu Yokota, Andrea Bizzego, et al. 2022. "A Method to Soothe and Promote Sleep in Crying Infants Utilizing the Transport Response." *Current Biology* 32, no. 20: P4521–29. https://doi.org/10.1016/j.cub.2022.08.041.

32. Markell, Jenny. n.d. "Can Listening to Music Improve Your Workout?" National Center for Health Research. https://www.center4research.org/can-listening-music-improve-workout/.

33. Delgado, Jennifer. n.d. "Science Confirms: Dancing Makes You Happy." *Psychology Spot* (blog). https://psychology-spot.com/dancing-makes-me-happy/#google_vignette.

34. Winkler, István, Gábor P. Háden, Olivia Ladinig, István Sziller, and Henkjan Honing. 2009. "Newborn Infants Detect the Beat in Music." *Proceedings of the National Academy of Sciences* 106, no. 7: 2468–71. https://doi.org/10.1073/pnas.0809035106.

35. Phillips-Silver, Jessica, and Laurel J. Trainor. 2005. "Feeling the Beat: Movement Influences Infant Rhythm Perception." *Science* 308, no. 5727: 1430. https://doi.org/10.1126/science.1110922.

36. Zentner, Marcel, and Tuomas Eerola. 2010. "Rhythmic Engagement with Music

in Infancy." *Proceedings of the National Academy of Sciences* 107, no. 13: 5768–73. https://doi.org/10.1073/pnas.1000121107.

37. Bullowa, Margaret. 1979. *Before Speech: The Beginning of Interpersonal Communication*. Cambridge: Cambridge University Press.

38. Fink, Bernhard, Bettina Bläsing, Andrea Ravignani, and Todd K. Shackelford. 2021. "Evolution and Functions of Human Dance." *Evolution and Human Behavior* 42, no. 4. https://doi.org/10.1016/j.evolhumbehav.2021.01.003.

39. Hagen, Edward H. 2022. "The Biological Roots of Music and Dance." *Human Nature* 33 (August): 261–79. https://doi.org/10.1007/s12110-022-09429-9.

40. Hannon, Erin E., Adena Schachner, and Jessica E. Nave-Blodgett. 2017. "Babies Know Bad Dancing When They See It: Older but Not Younger Infants Discriminate between Synchronous and Asynchronous Audiovisual Musical Displays." *Journal of Experimental Child Psychology* 159 (July): 159–74. https://doi.org/10.1016/j.jecp.2017.01.006.

41. Cirelli, Laura K., Stephanie J. Wan, and Laurel J. Trainor. 2014. "Fourteen-Month-Old Infants Use Interpersonal Synchrony as a Cue to Direct Helpfulness." *Philosophical Transactions of the Royal Society B: Biological Sciences* 369, no. 1658: 20130400. https://doi.org/10.1098/rstb.2013.0400.

42. Lense, Miriam D., Sarah Shultz, Corine Astésano, and Warren Jones. 2022. "Music of Infant-Directed Singing Entrains Infants' Social Visual Behavior." *Proceedings of the National Academy of Sciences* 119, no. 45: e2116967119. https://doi.org/10.1073/pnas.2116967119.

43. Yingying, Hou, Bei Song, Yinying Hu, Yafeng Pan, and Yi Hu. 2020. "The Averaged Inter-Brain Coherence between the Audience and a Violinist Predicts the Popularity of Violin Performance." *NeuroImage* 211 (May): 116655. https://doi.org/10.1016/j.neuroimage.2020.116655.

44. Hennig, Holger. 2014. "Synchronization in Human Musical Rhythms and Mutually Interacting Complex Systems." *Proceedings of the National Academy of Sciences* 111, no. 36: 12974–79. https://doi.org/10.1073/pnas.1324142111.

45. Gerry, David, Andrea Unrau, and Laurel J. Trainor. 2012. "Active Music Classes in Infancy Enhance Musical, Communicative and Social Development." *Developmental Science* 15, no. 3: 398–407. https://doi.org/10.1111/j.1467-7687.2012.01142.x.

46. Phillips-Silver, Jessica, and Laurel J. Trainor. 2005. "Feeling the Beat: Movement Influences Infant Rhythm Perception." *Science* 308, no. 5727: 1430. https://doi.org/10.1126/science.1110922.

47. Williamson, Selena, and Jacqueline M. McGrath. 2019. "What Are the Effects of the Maternal Voice on Preterm Infants in the NICU?" *Advances in Neonatal Care* 19, no. 4: 294–310. https://doi.org/10.1097/anc.0000000000000578.

48. Corbeil, Mariève, Sandra E. Trehub, and Isabelle Peretz. 2015. "Singing Delays the Onset of Infant Distress." *Infancy* 21, no. 3: 373–91. https://doi.org/10.1111/infa.12114.

49. Shenfield, Tali, Sandra E. Trehub, and Takayuki Nakata. 2003. "Maternal Singing Modulates Infant Arousal." *Psychology of Music* 31, no. 4: 365–75. https://doi.org/10.1177/03057356030314002.

50. Snow, Shelley, Nicolò Francesco Bernardi, Nilufar Sabet-Kassouf, Daniel Moran, and Alexandre Lehmann. 2018. "Exploring the Experience and Effects of Vocal Toning." *Journal of Music Therapy* 55, no. 2: 221–50. https://doi.org/10.1093/jmt/thy003.

51. Kraus, Michael W. 2017. "Voice-Only Communication Enhances Empathic Accuracy." *American Psychologist* 72, no. 7: 644–54. https://doi.org/10.1037/amp0000147.

52. Laplante, Debi, and Nalini Ambady. 2003. "On How Things Are Said: Voice Tone, Voice Intensity, Verbal Content, and Perceptions of Politeness." *Journal of Language and Social Psychology* 22, no. 4: 434–41. https://doi.org/10.1177/0261927X03258084.

53. Russel, Julia. 2023. "Visual Cliff Experiment (Gibson and Walk, 1960)." Simply Psychology. https://www.simplypsychology.org/visual-cliff-experiment.html.

54. Malviya, Shikha, Barbra Zupan, and Pamela Meredith. 2022. "Alternative Interventions in Clinical Mental Health Settings: A Survey of Mental Health Professionals' Perceptions." *Complementary Therapies in Clinical Practice* 49 (November): 101668. https://doi.org/10.1016/j.ctcp.2022.101668.

55. Pew Research Center Social & Demographic Trends Project. 2015. *Parenting in America: Satisfaction, Time and Support.* https://www.pewresearch.org/social-trends/2015/12/17/2-satisfaction-time-and-support/.

56. Miller, Claire Cain. 2018. "The Relentlessness of Modern Parenting." *New York Times,* December 25, 2018. https://www.nytimes.com/2018/12/25/upshot/the-relentlessness-of-modern-parenting.html.

57. Hammond, Ruth Anne. 2021. "Seeing Infants Differently: Magda Gerber's Contributions to the Early Care and Education Field and Their Continuing Relevance." *Early Child Development and Care* 191, no. 7–8: 1–14. https://doi.org/10.1080/03004430.2020.1865942.

58. Ibid.

59. Allen, Summer. 2018. "The Science of Awe." Greater Good Science Center at the University of California, Berkeley. https://ggsc.berkeley.edu/images/uploads/GGSC-JTF_White_Paper-Awe_FINAL.pdf.

60. Brown, Stuart L., and Christopher C. Vaughan. 2009. *Play: How It Shapes the Brain, Opens the Imagination, and Invigorates the Soul.* New York: Avery.

61. Magda Gerber Legacy. n.d. "On Their Own with Our Help." Magda Gerber Legacy. https://magdagerber.org/video/on-their-own-with-our-help/.

62. Feldman, Ruth. 2007. "Parent Infant Synchrony and the Construction of Shared Timing; Physiological Precursors, Developmental Outcomes, and Risk Conditions." *Journal of Child Psychology and Psychiatry* 48, no. 3–4: 329–54. https://doi.org/10.1111/j.1469-7610.2006.01701.x.

63. Beebe, Beatrice, and Miriam Steele. 2013. "How Does Microanalysis of Mother–Infant Communication Inform Maternal Sensitivity and Infant Attachment?" *Attachment & Human Development* 15, no. 5–6: 583–602. https://doi.org/10.1080/14616734.2013.841050.

64. Feldman, Ruth. 2007. "Parent Infant Synchrony and the Construction of Shared Timing; Physiological Precursors, Developmental Outcomes, and Risk Conditions." *Journal of Child Psychology and Psychiatry* 48, no. 3–4: 329–54. https://doi.org/10.1111/j.1469-7610.2006.01701.x.

65. Feldman, Ruth. 2003. "Infant-Mother and Infant-Father Synchrony: The Coregulation of Positive Arousal." *Infant Mental Health Journal* 24, no. 1: 1–23. https://doi.org/10.1002/imhj.10041.

66. Lents, Nathan H. 2017. "Why Play Is Important." *Psychology Today* (blog), May 1, 2017. https://www.psychologytoday.com/us/blog/beastly-behavior/201705/why-play-is-important.

67. Esseily, Rana, Lauriane Rat-Fischer, Eszter Somogyi, Kevin John O'Regan, and

Jacqueline Fagard. 2015. "Humour Production May Enhance Observational Learning of a New Tool-Use Action in 18-Month-Old Infants." *Cognition and Emotion* 30, no. 4: 817–25. https://doi.org/10.1080/02699931.2015.1036840.

68. Addyman, Caspar, Charlotte Fogelquist, Lenka Levakova, and Sarah Rees. 2018. "Social Facilitation of Laughter and Smiles in Preschool Children." *Frontiers in Psychology* 9 (June). https://doi.org/10.3389/fpsyg.2018.01048.

69. Ainsworth, Mary D. Salter, Silvia M. Bell, and Donelda J. Stayton. 1972. "Individual Differences in the Development of Some Attachment Behaviors." *Merrill-Palmer Quarterly of Behavior and Development* 18 (2): 123–43. https://www.jstor.org/stable/23083966.

70. Conboy, Barbara T., Rechele Brooks, Andrew N. Meltzoff, and Patricia K. Kuhl. 2015. "Social Interaction in Infants' Learning of Second-Language Phonetics: An Exploration of Brain-Behavior Relations." *Developmental Neuropsychology* 40, no. 4: 216–29. https://doi.org/10.1080/87565641.2015.1014487.

71. Lytle, Sarah Roseberry, Adrian Garcia-Sierra, and Patricia K. Kuhl. 2018. "Two Are Better than One: Infant Language Learning from Video Improves in the Presence of Peers." *Proceedings of the National Academy of Sciences* 115, no. 40: 9859–66. https://doi.org/10.1073/pnas.1611621115.

72. "Patricia Kuhl—The Social Brain 'Gates' Human Language Learning." YouTube video, 48:06. February 28, 2019. https://www.youtube.com/watch?v=sSH7fUjoOxM.

73. Vedantam, Shankar, Parth Shah, Tara Boyle, and Laura Kwerel. "Baby Talk: Decoding the Secret Language of Babies." NPR, September 30, 2019. https://www.npr.org/2019/09/30/765855335/baby-talk-decoding-the-secret-language-of-babies.

74. Goldstein, Michael H., and Jennifer A. Schwade. 2008. "Social Feedback to Infants' Babbling Facilitates Rapid Phonological Learning." *Psychological Science* 19, no. 5: 515–23. https://doi.org/10.1111/j.1467-9280.2008.02117.x.

75. Rice, Mae. 2019. "Here's Why You Unconsciously Copy Other People's Mannerisms." Discovery. August 1, 2019. https://www.discovery.com/science/copy-other-peoples-mannerisms.

76. Sauciuc, Gabriela-Alina, Jagoda Zlakowska, Tomas Persson, Sara Lenninger, and Elainie Alenkaer Madsen. 2020. "Imitation Recognition and Its Prosocial Effects in 6-Month Old Infants." *PLOS One* 15, no. 5: e0232717. https://doi.org/10.1371/journal.pone.0232717.

77. Pelaez, Martha, Javier Virues-Ortega, and Jacob L. Gewirtz. 2011. "Reinforcement of Vocalizations through Contingent Vocal Imitation." *Journal of Applied Behavior Analysis* 44, no. 1: 33–40. https://doi.org/10.1901/jaba.2011.44-33.

78. Jasnow, Michael, and Stanley Feldstein. 1986. "Adult-like Temporal Characteristics of Mother-Infant Vocal Interactions." *Child Development* 57, no. 3: 754–61. https://pubmed.ncbi.nlm.nih.gov/3720401/.

79. Bigelow, Ann E., and Michelle Power. 2022. "Influences of Infants' and Mothers' Contingent Vocal Responsiveness on Young Infants' Vocal Social Bids in the Still Face Task." *Infant Behavior and Development* 69 (November): 101776. https://doi.org/10.1016/j.infbeh.2022.101776.

80. Masur, Elise Frank, and Janet Olson. 2008. "Mothers' and Infants' Responses to Their Partners' Spontaneous Action and Vocal/Verbal Imitation." *Infant Behavior and Development* 31, no. 4: 704–15. https://doi.org/10.1016/j.infbeh.2008.04.005.

81. Fernald, Anne. 1985. "Four-Month-Old Infants Prefer to Listen to Motherese." *Infant Behavior and Development* 8, no. 2: 181–95. https://doi.org/10.1016/s0163 -6383(85)80005-9.

82. Eckart, Kim. 2020. "Not Just 'Baby Talk': Parentese Helps Parents, Babies Make 'Conversation' and Boosts Language Development." Press release, February 3, 2020. https://www.washington.edu/news/2020/02/03/not-just-baby -talk-parentese-helps-parents-babies-make-conversation-and-boosts-language -development/.

83. Ramírez-Esparza, Nairán, Adrián García-Sierra, and Patricia K. Kuhl. 2017. "Look Who's Talking NOW! Parentese Speech, Social Context, and Language Development across Time." *Frontiers in Psychology* 8 (June). https://doi.org/10.3389/ fpsyg.2017.01008.

84. Brink, Susan. "Scholars Confirm What Itsy Bitsy Babies around the World Already Know." NPR, August 14, 2022. https://www.npr.org/sections/goatsand soda/2022/08/14/1116524222/scholars-confirm-what-itsy-bitsy-babies-around -the-world-already-know.

85. Brandt, Anthony, Molly Gebrian, and L. Robert Slevc. 2012. "Music and Early Language Acquisition." *Frontiers in Psychology* 3 (327). https://doi.org/10.3389/fpsyg .2012.00327.

86. Goldstein, Michael H., and Jennifer A. Schwade. 2008. "Social Feedback to Infants' Babbling Facilitates Rapid Phonological Learning." *Psychological Science* 19, no. 5: 515–23. https://doi.org/10.1111/j.1467-9280.2008.02117.x.

87. Ramsdell-Hudock, Heather L., Anne S. Warlaumont, Lindsey E. Foss, and Candice Perry. 2019. "Classification of Infant Vocalizations by Untrained Listeners." *Journal of Speech, Language, and Hearing Research* 62, no. 9: 3265–75. https://doi.org/10 .1044/2019_jslhr-s-18-0494.

88. Gros-Louis, Julie, Meredith J. West, and Andrew P. King. 2014. "Maternal Responsiveness and the Development of Directed Vocalizing in Social Interactions." *Infancy* 19, no. 4: 385–408. https://doi.org/10.1111/infa.12054.

89. Goldstein, Michael H., and Jennifer A. Schwade. 2008. "Social Feedback to Infants' Babbling Facilitates Rapid Phonological Learning." *Psychological Science* 19, no. 5: 515–23. https://doi.org/10.1111/j.1467-9280.2008.02117.x.

90. Gros-Louis, Julie, Meredith J. West, and Andrew P. King. 2014. "Maternal Responsiveness and the Development of Directed Vocalizing in Social Interactions." *Infancy* 19, no. 4: 385–408. https://doi.org/10.1111/infa.12054.

91. Friederici, Angela D. 2006. "The Neural Basis of Language Development and Its Impairment." *Neuron* 52, no. 6: 941–52. https://doi.org/10.1016/j.neuron.2006 .12.002.

92. Brandt, Anthony, Molly Gebrian, and L. Robert Slevc. 2012. "Music and Early Language Acquisition." *Frontiers in Psychology* 3, no. 327. https://doi.org/10.3389/ fpsyg.2012.00327.

93. Kotilahti, Kalle, Ilkka Nissilä, Tiina Näsi, Lauri Lipiäinen, Tommi Noponen, Pekka Meriläinen, Minna Huotilainen, and Vineta Fellman. 2010. "Hemodynamic Responses to Speech and Music in Newborn Infants." *Human Brain Mapping* 31, no. 4: 499–668. https://doi.org/10.1002/hbm.20890.

94. Pino, Maria Chiara, Marco Giancola, and Simonetta D'Amico. 2023. "The Association between Music and Language in Children: A State-of-the-Art Review." *Children* 10, no. 5: 801. https://doi.org/10.3390/children10050801.

95. Kuhl, Patricia K., Jean E. Andruski, Inna A. Chistovich, Ludmilla A. Chistovich, Elena V. Kozhevnikova, Viktoria L. Ryskina, Elvira I. Stolyarova, Ulla Sundberg, and Francisco Lacerda. 1997. "Cross-Language Analysis of Phonetic Units in Language Addressed to Infants." *Science* 277, no. 5326: 684–86. https://doi.org/10 .1126/science.277.5326.684.

96. Prather, Jonathan F., Kazuo Okanoya, and Johan J. Bolhuis. 2017. "Brains for Birds and Babies: Neural Parallels between Birdsong and Speech Acquisition." *Neuroscience & Biobehavioral Reviews* 81 (October): 225–37. https://doi.org/10.1016/j .neubiorev.2016.12.035.

97. Brandt, Anthony, et al. 2012. "Music and Early Language Acquisition." *Frontiers in Psychology* 3, no. 327. https://doi.org/10.3389/fpsyg.2012.00327.

98. Aslaksen, Karoline, and Håvard Lorås. 2018. "The Modality-Specific Learning Style Hypothesis: A Mini-Review." *Frontiers in Psychology* 9 (August). https://doi .org/10.3389/fpsyg.2018.01538.

99. Rains, Jenny R., Catherine Ann Kelly, and Robert L. Durham. 2008. "The Evolution of the Importance of Multi-Sensory Teaching Techniques in Elementary Mathematics: Theory and Practice." *Journal of Theory and Practice in Education* 4, no. 2: 239–52. https://dergipark.org.tr/tr/download/article-file/63273.

100. Bahrick, Lorraine E., and Robert Lickliter. 2000. "Intersensory Redundancy Guides Attentional Selectivity and Perceptual Learning in Infancy." *Developmental Psychology* 36, no. 2: 190–201. https://doi.org/10.1037//0012-1649.36.2.190.

101. Thiessen, Erik D., and Jenny R. Saffran. 2009. "How the Melody Facilitates the Message and Vice Versa in Infant Learning and Memory." *Annals of the New York Academy of Sciences* 1169, no. 1: 225–33. https://doi.org/10.1111/j.1749-6632.2009 .04547.x.

102. Goodwyn, Susan W., Linda P. Acredolo, and Catherine A. Brown. 2000. "Impact of Symbolic Gesturing on Early Language Development." *Journal of Nonverbal Behavior* 24, no. 2: 81–103. https://doi.org/10.1023/a:1006653828895.

103. Masataka, Nobuo. 1992. "Motherese in a Signed Language." *Infant Behavior and Development* 15, no. 4: 453–60. https://doi.org/10.1016/0163-6383(92)80013-k.

104. Jimenez, Manuel E., Alan L. Mendelsohn, Yong Lin, Patricia Shelton, and Nancy Reichman. 2019. "Early Shared Reading Is Associated with Less Harsh Parenting." *Journal of Developmental & Behavioral Pediatrics* 40, no. 7: 530–37. https://doi.org/10 .1097/DBP.0000000000000687.

105. Jusczyk, Peter W., and Elizabeth A. Hohne. 1997. "Infants' Memory for Spoken Words." *Science* 277, no. 5334: 1984–86. https://doi.org/10.1126/science.277.5334 .1984.

106. Horst, Jessica S. 2013. "Context and Repetition in Word Learning." *Frontiers in Psychology* 4, no. 149. https://doi.org/10.3389/fpsyg.2013.00149.

107. Jimenez, Manuel E., Nancy E. Reichman, Colter Mitchell, Lisa Schneper, Sara McLanahan, and Daniel A. Notterman. 2020. "Shared Reading at Age 1 Year and Later Vocabulary: A Gene–Environment Study." *The Journal of Pediatrics* 216 (January): 189–96. https://doi.org/10.1016/j.jpeds.2019.07.008.

108. Papadimitriou, Aspasia, Catherine Smyth, Nina Politimou, Fabia Franco, and Lauren Stewart. 2021. "The Impact of the Home Musical Environment on Infants' Language Development." *Infant Behavior and Development* 65 (November): 101651. https://doi.org/10.1016/j.infbeh.2021.101651.

109. Dondena, Chiara, Valentina Riva, Massimo Molteni, Gabriella Musacchia, and Chiara Cantiani. 2021. "Impact of Early Rhythmic Training on Language Acquisition and Electrophysiological Functioning Underlying Auditory Processing: Feasibility and Preliminary Findings in Typically Developing Infants." *Brain Sciences* 11, no. 11: 1546. https://doi.org/10.3390/brainsci11111546.

110. Zhao, T. Christina, and Patricia K. Kuhl. 2016. "Musical Intervention Enhances Infants' Neural Processing of Temporal Structure in Music and Speech." *Proceedings of the National Academy of Sciences* 113, no. 19: 5212–17. https://doi.org/10.1073/pnas.1603984113.

111. Chorna, Olena D., James C. Slaughter, Lulu Wang, Ann R. Stark, and Nathalie L. Maitre. 2014. "A Pacifier-Activated Music Player with Mother's Voice Improves Oral Feeding in Preterm Infants." *Pediatrics* 133, no. 3: 462–68. https://doi.org/10.1542/peds.2013-2547.

112. Dziewolska, Halina, and Joseph Cautilli. 2005. "Brief Report: The Reinforcing Effects of Paternal Verbal Stimulation and Gentle Pushing on Kicking Behavior in a 36 Week Old In-Utero Fetus: A Partial Replication and a Cautionary Note." *The Behavior Analyst Today* 6, no. 3: 163–65. https://doi.org/10.1037/h0100064.

113. Perry, Nina. 2013. "The Universal Language of Lullabies." *BBC News*, January 21, 2013. https://www.bbc.com/news/magazine-21035103.

114. MacKinlay, Elizabeth, and Felicity Baker. 2005. "Nurturing Herself, Nurturing Her Baby: Creating Positive Experiences for First-Time Mothers through Lullaby Singing." *Women and Music: A Journal of Gender and Culture* 9, no. 1: 69–89. https://muse.jhu.edu/pub/17/article/190642/summary.

115. Loewy, Joanne, Kristen Stewart, Ann-Marie Dassler, Aimee Telsey, and Peter Homel. 2013. "The Effects of Music Therapy on Vital Signs, Feeding, and Sleep in Premature Infants." *Pediatrics* 131, no. 5: 902–18. https://doi.org/10.1542/peds.2012-1367.

116. Coleman, Jacquelyn Michelle, Rosalie Rebollo Pratt, Ronald A. Stoddard, Dale R. Gerstmann, and Hans-Hennin Abel. 1997. The Effects of the Male and Female Singing and Speaking Voices on Selected Physiological and Behavioral Measures of Premature Infants in the Intensive Care Unit. *International Journal of Arts Medicine* 5, no. 2: 4–11.

117. Persico, Giuseppina, Laura Antolini, Patrizia Vergani, Walter Costantini, Maria Teresa Nardi, and Lidia Bellotti. 2017. "Maternal Singing of Lullabies during Pregnancy and after Birth: Effects on Mother–Infant Bonding and on Newborns' Behaviour. Concurrent Cohort Study." *Women and Birth* 30, no. 4: e214–20. https://doi.org/10.1016/j.wombi.2017.01.007.

118. Wulff, Verena, Philip Hepp, Oliver T. Wolf, Tanja Fehm, and Nora K. Schaal. 2021. "The Influence of Maternal Singing on Well-Being, Postpartum Depression and Bonding–A Randomised, Controlled Trial." *BMC Pregnancy and Childbirth* 21, no 501. https://doi.org/10.1186/s12884-021-03933-z.

119. Lense, Miriam D., Sarah Shultz, Corine Astésano, and Warren Jones. 2022. "Music of Infant-Directed Singing Entrains Infants' Social Visual Behavior." *Proceedings of the National Academy of Sciences* 119, no. 45. https://doi.org/10.1073/pnas.2116967119.

120. Namjoo, Razyeh, Roghayeh Mehdipour-Rabori, Behnaz Bagherian, and Monirsadat Nematollahi. 2022. "Comparing the Effectiveness of Mother's Live Lullaby

and Recorded Lullaby on Physiological Responses and Sleep of Preterm Infants: A Clinical Trial Study." *Journal of Complementary and Integrative Medicine* 19 (1): 121–29. https://doi.org/10.1515/jcim-2020-0507.

121. Mariève Corbeil, Sandra E. Trehub, and Isabelle Peretz. 2015. "Singing Delays the Onset of Infant Distress." *Infancy* 21, no. 3: 373–91, https://doi.org/10.1111/infa .12114.

122. Ilari, Beatriz, and Megha Sundara. 2009. "Music Listening Preferences in Early Life." *Journal of Research in Music Education* 56, no. 4: 357–69. https://doi.org/10 .1177/0022429408329107.

123. Trainor, Laurel J., Elissa D. Clark, Anita Huntley, and Beth A. Adams. 1997. "The Acoustic Basis of Preferences for Infant-Directed Singing." *Infant Behavior and Development* 20, no. 3: 383–96. https://doi.org/10.1016/s0163-6383(97)90009-6.

124. Trehub, Sandra E., Anna M. Unyk, Stuart B. Kamenetsky, David S. Hill, Laurel J. Trainor, Jo L. Henderson, and Myra Saraza. 1997. "Mothers' and Fathers' Singing to Infants." *Developmental Psychology* 33, no. 3: 500–507. https://doi.org/10 .1037//0012-1649.33.3.500.

125. Shapiro, Ari, Lauren Hodges, and Ashley Brown. 2022. "Your Everyday Rituals Do Impact Your Life — Just Not How You Might Expect." NPR, September 14, 2022. https://www.npr.org/2022/09/14/1122488496/rituals-book-covid -graduation-birthdays-anthropology.

126. Bell, Catherine M. 1992. *Ritual Theory, Ritual Practice*. New York: Oxford University Press.

127. Charles, Sarah J., Valerie van Mulukom, Jennifer E. Brown, Fraser Watts, Robin I. M. Dunbar, and Miguel Farias. 2021. "United on Sunday: The Effects of Secular Rituals on Social Bonding and Affect." *PLOS One* 16, no. 1: e0242546. https://doi .org/10.1371/journal.pone.0242546.

128. Cherry, Kendra. 2024. "How Listening to Music Can Have Psychological Benefits." Verywell Mind. Last modified April 24, 2024. https://www.verywellmind .com/surprising-psychological-benefits-of-music-4126866.

129. Mualem, Orit, and Pnina S. Klein. 2013. "The Communicative Characteristics of Musical Interactions Compared with Play Interactions between Mothers and Their One-Year-Old Infants." *Early Child Development and Care* 183, no. 7: 899–915. https:// doi.org/10.1080/03004430.2012.688824.

130. Kirby, Anna L., Mariam Dahbi, Sarah Surrain, Meredith L. Rowe, and Gigi Luk. 2022. "Music Uses in Preschool Classrooms in the U.S.: A Multiple-Methods Study." *Early Childhood Education Journal* 51 (February): 515–29. https://doi.org/10 .1007/s10643-022-01309-2.

131. Tsang, Christine D., Simone Falk, and Alexandria Hessel. 2016. "Infants Prefer Infant-Directed Song over Speech." *Child Development* 88, no. 4: 1207–15. https://doi .org/10.1111/cdev.12647.

132. Lebedeva, Gina C., and Patricia K. Kuhl. 2010. "Sing That Tune: Infants' Perception of Melody and Lyrics and the Facilitation of Phonetic Recognition in Songs." *Infant Behavior and Development* 33, no. 4: 419–30. https://doi.org/10.1016/j .infbeh.2010.04.006.

133. Cooper, Robin Panneton, Jane Abraham, Sheryl Berman, and Margaret Staska. 1997. "The Development of Infants' Preference for Motherese." *Infant Behavior and Development* 20, no. 4: 477–88. https://doi.org/10.1016/s0163-6383(97)90037-0.

134. Fernald, Anne, Traute Taeschner, Judy Dunn, Mechthild Papousek, Bénédicte de Boysson-Bardies, and Ikuko Fukui. 1989. "A Cross-Language Study of Prosodic Modifications in Mothers' and Fathers' Speech to Preverbal Infants." *Journal of Child Language* 16, no. 3: 477–501. https://doi.org/10.1017/s0305000900010679.

135. Janata, Petr. 2009. "The Neural Architecture of Music-Evoked Autobiographical Memories." *Cerebral Cortex* 19, no. 11: 2579–94. https://doi.org/10.1093/cercor/bhp008.

136. Kołomańska-Bogucka, Daria, and Agnieszka Irena Mazur-Bialy. 2019. "Physical Activity and the Occurrence of Postnatal Depression—a Systematic Review." *Medicina* 55, no. 9: 560. https://doi.org/10.3390/medicina55090560.

137. Lee, Ling Ling, Caroline. A. Mulvaney, Yoko Kin Yoke Wong, Edwin S. Y. Chan, Michael C. Watson, and Hui Hsin Lin. 2021. "Walking for Hypertension." Cochrane Database of Systematic Reviews. https://doi.org/10.1002/14651858.CD008823.pub2.

138. Mualem, Raed, Gerry Leisman, Yusra Zbedat, Sherif Ganem, Ola Mualem, Monjed Amaria, Aiman Kozle, Safa Khayat-Moughrabi, and Alon Ornai. 2018. "The Effect of Movement on Cognitive Performance." *Frontiers in Public Health* 6 (April). https://doi.org/10.3389/fpubh.2018.00100.

139. Kemp, Nicola, and Jo Josephidou. 2023. "Babies and Toddlers Outdoors: A Narrative Review of the Literature on Provision for under Twos in ECEC Settings." *Early Years* 43, no. 1: 137–50. https://doi.org/10.1080/09575146.2021.1915962.

140. Roslund, Marja I., Riikka Puhakka, Mira Grönroos, Noora Nurminen, Sami Oikarinen, Ahmad M. Gazali, Ondřej Cinek, et al. 2020. "Biodiversity Intervention Enhances Immune Regulation and Health-Associated Commensal Microbiota among Daycare Children." *Science Advances* 6, no. 42: eaba2578. https://doi.org/10.1126/sciadv.aba2578.

141. Harrison, Yvonne. 2004. "The Relationship between Daytime Exposure to Light and Night-Time Sleep in 6–12-Week-Old Infants." *Journal of Sleep Research* 13, no. 4: 345–52. https://doi.org/10.1111/j.1365-2869.2004.00435.x.

142. Taniguchi, Keita, Mayuko Takano, Yui Tobari, Motoshi Hayano, Shinichiro Nakajima, Masaru Mimura, Kazuo Tsubota, and Yoshihiro Noda. 2022. "Influence of External Natural Environment Including Sunshine Exposure on Public Mental Health: A Systematic Review." *Psychiatry International* 3, no. 1: 91–113. https://doi.org/10.3390/psychiatryint3010008.

143. Tao, Dan, Yang Gao, Alistair Cole, Julien S. Baker, Yaodong Gu, Rashmi Supriya, Tomas K. Tong, Qiuli Hu, and Roger Awan-Scully. 2022. "The Physiological and Psychological Benefits of Dance and Its Effects on Children and Adolescents: A Systematic Review." *Frontiers in Physiology* 13 (925958). https://doi.org/10.3389/fphys.2022.925958.

INDEX

A

Accentuating music, 163–164
Accountable activities, 195–196
Actions, based on assumptions, 61, 62
Addyman, Caspar, 137
Ainsworth, Mary, 24, 143
    research model devised by, 25
    secure attachment and, 25–26
    Strange Situation studies created by,
        63
Airway obstructions, rocking and
        bouncing of baby, in decreasing, 72
Albert, Rachel, 149
Alignment, 104
Allodynia, 84
Andrews, Julie, 213
Animals
    feelings of, 97
    learning of social skills, 132
Anticipation face, 138
Anxiety
    music in reducing, 73
Arms, erratic/jagged movements of, 48
Assumptions, 66
    actions based on, 61, 62, 66

Attachment
    doing behaviors, 28
    improving to baby, 29
    secure, 14–15, 25–26, 28
    strengthening your muscle in, 29,
        30–31
    theory on, 15, 24, 25, 43, 44
    types of, 25
Attachment gym, lack of time for, 33
Attachment parenting, 29
Auditory modality, 164, 165
Austin, Diane, 86
Authenticity, 99
    of play, 142

B

Babble Boosts
    reading into sounds, 159–160
    singing your speech, 156–158
    vocal mirroring as, 150–155
Babies. See also Newborns
    bedtime cues of, 52
    body language of, 62
    bouncing of, while standing, 71
    building secure attachment with, 14–15

Babies (*continued*)
   caring for, 106–107
   cognitive development of, 133
   communication with, 41
   creating space with, 38
   crying by, 87
   desire for singing, 224
   determining what is bothering,
      43–44
   developing language of play with,
      128–144
   development of games and growth
      of, 139
   development of language in, 145–172
   as dogs, 177–178
   driving with, 83–86
   experiencing fully, 37
   in the Explorer State, 118–119, 126
   Explorer State in, 122–123
   feeling in sync with, 12
   feelings of, 125
   fussiness of, 55–56, 69–70
   getting cues from the average, 46–47
   having communication with using
      sounds, 13
   heartbeat of, 73–74
   helping go from music to meaning,
      163–164
   home base for, 26–27
   ideal times for learning cues of,
      51–52
   importance of connection to, 25
   improving attachment to, 29
   increasing communication with, 12
   laughter of, 133, 137
   learning through repetition, 134–135
   listening to, 63–66
   matching energy of, 142–143
   mirroring vocals of, 155
   modes of being with, 117–118
   morning song as signal for, 202–203
   moving to beat in, 74–75
   needs of, 63–64, 70, 115
   playing with, 113–127, 143
   problem approach to, 13
   reactions to stress, 100–101
   reading to, 168–169
   repeating sounds of, 151
   responding to music by, 73

   responding to needs of, 29, 66
   rocking of, 72
   singing to, 84, 199
   social skills for, 133
   soothing of, 12, 69–70, 78–81,
      88–91, 109
   speaking language of, 37, 40–56
   symbolic function in, 180–181
   taking care of new, 9–17
   talking about change with, 226–229
   temperament of, 63
   understanding mental state of, 44
   using voice to soothe, 88–91
   vocalizations of, 151
Baby blues, 54–55
Baby Buddha Massage, 36–37, 69
Baby in Tune, 14, 78
   classes for, 15, 21
Baby time zone, 154
Bareilles, Sara, 90
Beastly Behavior (Lents), 132–133
Beat
   of bonding, 77–78
   moving to a, 70
   tapping to a, 80–81
"Beautiful Betty," 88
Bedtime
   clues for, 56
   doing successful fade-out at, 187–188
   making a Bubble Moment, 224
   making more enjoyable, 12, 192–193
Beebe, Beatrice, 130–131
Behavior
   attachment, 28
   dancing and social, 76
   lullabies and, 178–179
Bell, Catherine, 197
Bells in rituals, 206
Beyoncé, 86, 163
Blanks, leaving, 169
Body language, 40–56, 62, 97
Body movements, fluid, 50
Bonding, 143
   beat of, 77–78
   creation of, 76
Bouncing
   to the rhythm, 93
   in sync with a song, 79
Bowlby, John, 24–25, 28, 117

Brain activation, 162
Brandt, Anthony, 162–163
Brazelton, Berry, 27, 46, 117
Breaths, taking deep, 89, 93, 102
Brown, Brené, 64
Brown, Stuart, 123
Bubble Moments, 16, 17, 32, 129, 148, 153, 182, 223–229
    Baby Buddha Massage as, 36–37, 39
    baby calm moment, 110
    Baby Fish Mouth, 139
    bedtime clues, 56
    creating, 15–16, 20–66
    Dance Party, 222
    as enjoyable, 225
    Explorer State, 127
    Eye See You, 51
    Fade-outs, 188
    getting through tough moments, 225
    Grounding Song, 219
    missing, 23–24
    Morning Song, 212
    opening space for, 41
    pauses, 66
    Puppet Play, 144
    setting the scene for, 21–39
    sign and sign, 171
    soothing, 79, 95
    tapping a beat, 81–82
    timing of, 32
    vocal mirror, 161
    wind-down, 193

C
Call and response, 151
Canonical speech, 159
Cappellas, 185
Caretaker, role of, 58
Chameleon effect, 150
Classic conditioning, 177
Communication, increasing with your baby, 12
Conditioning, classic, 177
Connection, importance of, to baby, 24–25
Connection booster, 220
Conversationalist, being a good, 149
Conversations
    being a hog in, 154–155

having, 151–152
    sparking, 152–154
Cooke, Sam, 90
Coordinating movements, 75
Creativity, 138, 141
Crying, 87
Cues
    determination of, 52–53
    getting from average baby, 46–47
    ideal times for learning baby's, 51–52
    lullabies as perfect, 179–183
    at night, 52
    noticing subtle, 41–42, 47–49, 50, 53–55
Curiosity, 38, 44–45

D
Dad effect, 138
Daily synchrony, 130–131
Dancing
    as beneficial, 75, 76, 220–222
    need for music in, 72
    social behavior and, 76
Dancing gene, 75
Depression
    music in reducing, 73
    postpartum, 54–55
Diaper-changing rituals, 203–205
Distance, choice of, in sparking conversation, 152–154
Distractions, 54
    limiting, 38
Dogs
    babies as, 177–178
    work of Pavlov with, 176–177, 190
Driving with baby, 83–86
Dubnoff School, Pilot Infant Program at the, 115
Dynamics, 157

E
Elton John, 86
Emotions
    home base as concept of, 26–27
    showing, 169
Empathy, 66
Endorphins, 73
Energy, matching baby's, 142–143

Enrichment, 143
Entrainment, 77, 182
Everyday activities, making less boring
    and more bonding, 194–214
Excitement, 136
Exercise, voice, 92
Expectations, coming without, 38
Experts, practicing with, 91
Explore, willingness to, 50
Explorer State, babies in, 118–119,
    122–123, 125, 126
    benefits of, 126
Eyebrows, 48
Eye contact
    maintaining, 50
Eye-to-eye gaze, avoiding, 47–48

F
Facial expression, relaxation of, 50,
    99, 103
Fade-out, 186–189, 190, 193
    evaluation of, 188–189
Faking, 100–101
Feeding rituals, 205–206
Feelings
    of babies, 125
    connected, 76
    getting to the bottom of a, 58–60
    showing your, 97–99
Feldman, Ruth, 131, 132
Focusing on the micro, 105
Four-step soothing method, 93
Frankl, Viktor, 64–65
Fun
    benefits of, 165–166
    making play, 141
Fussiness of babies, 55–56, 69–70

G
Games, types of, 134
Gaze
    avoiding eye-to-eye, 47–48
    shifting of, 147
Gebrian, Molly, 162–163
Gene, dancing, 75
Gerber, Magda, 115, 116–17, 119, 120,
    124

Gestures, 165
    hand, 165, 166, 171–172
    pauses between, 136, 166
Getting dressed rituals, 207–208
Gigs, starting with small, 90–91
Good-enough mothers, 28
"Good Morning My Love" (song), 21
Goodnight Moon, 168
Gopnik, Alison, 125
Gripping, 49
Grooving, 75–76
Grounding song, 216–219
Grounding through senses, 36
Group, power of a, 91, 93–94

H
Habits
    sound sleep, 175–193
Half Chorus, 190
Hammond, 116
Hand gestures in song, 165, 166, 171–
    172
Hawking, Stephen, 88
Heartbeat
    rhythm of, 73–74
    synchronization of, 71
"Hello" (song), 40
Hello voice exercise, 92
Help, asking for, 105–106
Home, setting up video camera in your,
    27–28
Home base, as emotional concept,
    26–27
Homo Ludens (Huizinga), 130
Hook
    lullabies as the, 179
    noticing the, 158
Huizinga, Johan, 130
Hunger, 46

I
Infants. See also Babies; Newborns
    preterm, 84–85
Inner state, 106
Intention to engage, 132
Interactive play, 129–130
Intervention, timing of, 124

K
Kangaroo care, 70
Kind, being to self, 38, 105
Kinesthetic modality, 164, 165
Kuhl, Patricia, 146–148, 170

L
Lady Gaga, 86
Language
    acquisition of, 146–147
    body, 40–56, 62, 97
    creating your own, 170
    development of, 145–172
    making music in development of,
        169–170
    musicality of, 157
    speaking baby's, 37, 40–56
Laughter, learning and, 133
Lead, resistance of urge to, 123
Learning
    laughter and, 133
    use of music for, 198
Legs, erratic/jagged movement of, 48
Lents, Nathan H., 132–133
Lip, jutting out of, 48
Listening, 57–66
    to babies, 57–66
    empathizing and, 66
    getting to bottom of, 58–60
    importance of, 58
    need for responses on, 61–63
    needs of baby and, 63–64, 66
    observations and, 60–61
    to questions, 59
    reactions and, 64–65
Lullabies, 175, 178–179. *See also*
        Singing
    bedtime, naps and, 183
    characteristics of, 183
    common FAQs, 190–191
    fade-out of, 188–189
    as family tune, 184
    as hook, 179
    as perfect cue, 179–183
    selection of, 183–184
    singing, 185–186
    as soothing, 179–180
    as transitional objects, 191
    wind-down in, 189–190
    writing, 184

M
Mahler, Margaret, 227–228
Mandarin, exposing babies to, 146–147
Mantras, 102
Massage, Baby Buddha, 36–37
Melody, reading with, 166–169
"Mentalizing" moments, rewarding
        your, 45
Mental/physical health inventory,
        104–106
    alignment in, 104
    asking for help, 105–106
    kindness in, 105
    sleep in, 104
Mental presence, 120–121
Mental state, reflecting your, 45–46
Messinger, Daniel, 131
Metronome, 72
Micro, focusing on the, 105
Mindfulness, 73
Mirror vocals, 148, 150–155, 160
Mitchell, Elizabeth, 215
Mitchell, Joni, 88
Moment, seizing the, 149
Morning
    as opportunity for reset, 201
    rituals in, 200–203
Morning song, as signal to baby, 202–203
Motherese, 209
Mothering, re-calibrating, 13
Mothers, good-enough, 28
Movements
    coordinating, 75
    smiling and, 74
    synchronous, 76, 77
Muscles
    building attachment, 30–31
    developing, 29
Music. *See also* Lullabies; Singing; Songs
    accentuating, 163–164
    benefits of, 73
    inconsistencies in the rhythm of for-
        eign, 74

Music (*continued*)
   in language development, 169–170
   movement to, 74–75
   need for in dancing, 72
   power of, 180
   predictability of, 198
   responding to, 73
   use of, for transitions and learning, 198
   virtualization with, 200
Musicality of language, 157

N
National Institute for Play, 123
Needs
   of babies, 63–64, 70, 115
   meeting own, 53–54
Newborns. *See also* Babies
   need for soothing, 70
Notes, rocking between two, 93
Nursing, in soothing baby, 69
Nurturance, psychological need for, 24

O
Observations, 60–61, 120
   asking questions and, 65
"One Day" (song), 39
On Their Own with Our Help (Gerber), 124
Openness, 138
Outdoors, Great, 219–220
Overstimulation, 46

P
Pacifiers, 177
   in soothing baby, 69
Pages, skipping, 168
Parent(s)
   feeling more like a, 12
   perceptions of play, 114
Parental reflective functioning (PRF),
   43–44, 45
Parentese, 156–157, 166, 209, 210
Parent-infant synchrony, 130–131, 132
Parenting, 29
   attachment, 29
   responsive, 29
*Parenting Mistakes through the Eyes of an
   Eight-Year Old*, 139–140

Parenting superpower, 108–110
   activating your, 96–110
   developing, 44–46
Part, playing the, 168
Pauses, 59, 65, 124, 136
Pavlov, Ivan Petrovich, work of, with
   dogs, 176–177, 190
"Peace Like a River" (song), 215
Perfect Pastimes, 16
"Perfect Paul," 88
Phrases, taking deep breaths between,
   93, 102
Pikler, Emmi, 115
Pilot Infant Program at the Dubnoff
   School, 115
Pitch, lowering of voice, 49
Pitching, 49
Play, 113, 129
   authenticity of, 142
   dad effect in, 138
   defining, 130
   developing language of, 128–144
   interactive, 129–130
   as a magic wand, 139–140
   making fun, 141
   parents' perceptions of, 114
   puppet, 144
   reasons for, 143
   synchrony of, 131–132
   tickle monster effect and, 135
   turning into activities you enjoy, 12
   willingness to, 50
*Play: How It Shapes the Brain, Open
   Imagination, and Invigorates the Soul*
   (Brown), 123
Playing, 113
   with time, 133–134
Playing and Reality (Winnicott), 30
Playmates, 136–137
Poppins, Mary, 212
Positive emotional arousal, 197
Positive interaction, 132
Positive psychology, 34
Post-baby system alert, 103
Postpartum depression, 54–55
Potential space, 30
Power of responses, 64–65

Preschool teacher technique, 176
Present, being, 32–33
Preterm infants, 84–85
Prime Bubble Moment, 182
Private jokes, 143
Problem approach to baby, 13
Prolonged synchrony, 132
Props, 138
Protection, psychological need for, 24
Psychological needs, 24
Puppet play, 144

Q
Questions
    asking, 59, 65
    listening to, 59

R
Reactions
    listening and, 64–65
    power of, 64–65
Readiness, communication of, 153
Reading
    to baby, 168–169
    with melody, 166–169
    sounds and, 148, 159–160
Reflective functioning, 44
Relaxation, 113–127
    of facial expression, 50, 99, 103
Remedy to Routine, 16
Repetition, 134–135, 164, 165, 167
Research on connection, 24–25
Resistance of urge to lead, 123
Respect, 116–117
Responses, need for in listening, 61–63
Responsive parenting, 29
Rhythm
    activities and, 69–82
    bouncing to, 78–79
    importance of, 70
    rocking of baby to, 72
    soothing of baby through, 78–81
Rihanna, 220
Ritualization, 196–200
Rituals, 196–200
    diaper-changing, 203–205
    feeding, 205–206

    getting dressed, 207–208
    going from routines to, 211
    morning, 200–203
    separation, 206–207
Ritual Theory, Ritual Practice (Bell), 197
Rocking to the rhythm, 72
Routine
    going to ritual from, 211
    making smoother and more fun, 12

S
Safety, psychological need for, 24
Saltman, Bethany, 28
Satisfaction, 136
Scene, setting for Bubble Moments,
    21–39
Secrets to soothing, 16, 68–110
Secure attachment, 25–26
    See Social behavior, dancing and, 76
Senses
    experiencing your, 38
    grounding through, 36
    involving, 164–166
Separation-individuation, 227
Separation rituals, 206–207
Serotonin, 220
Sheeran, Ed, 90
Singing, 90. See also Lullabies; Music;
    Songs
    abilities of, in singing lullabies, 176–
        177, 190
    benefits of, to baby, 84
    inabilities in, 212–214
    of lullabies, 185–186
    speed of, 102
    your speech, 148, 156–158, 160
Siri, 88
Slade, Arietta, 43
Sleep
    amount of, 104
    conditioning and, 177
    making bedtime more enjoyable,
        192–193
    songs for, 175
    soundness of, 175–193
Sleve, L. Robert, 162–163
Smiling, movement and, 74

Social context, 147
Social referencing, 97–98
Social school, 132–133
Social skills, learning of, by animals,
    132
Song(s). *See also* Music
    benefits of, for babies, 199
    bouncing to rhythm of a, 78–79
    distracting with a, 69
    grounding, 216–219
    hand gesturing in, 165, 166, 171–172
    lack of skills in writing, 209–211
    "One Day" as example of, 39
    using for important moments,
        206–207
    writing own, 13–14, 208–211
Soothing, 79., 93
    of babies, 12, 69–70, 78–81, 88–91,
        109
    four-step method of, 93
    secrets to, 16, 68–110
    successful methods of, 100, 101–102
Sounds
    conversations with baby using his, 13
    mirroring, 153
    reading into, 159–160
Space, creation of, 31, 38
Sparks, lighting the, 153–154
Speech
    canonical, 159
    simplifying your, 158
    singing your, 156–158
    slowing down your, 158
    speed of, 102
Standing, bouncing of baby while
    standing, 71
Standing up straight, 104
Staring contest, playing, 51
Stern, Daniel, 27, 117, 130
Stinginess, 48–49
Strange Situation, 25, 63
Stress, baby reactions to, 100–101
Stretching, committing to amount of,
    104
Striking, 49
Subtle cues, 41–42, 47–49, 50, 53–55
"Sweet Child o' Mine" (song), 183

Symbolic function, 180
Synchronization, 71, 76, 77, 81, 197
Synchrony
    daily, 130–131
    parent-infant, 130–131, 132
    of play, 131–132
Synthetic voices, 88

T
Tactile modality, 164, 165
Temperament of babies, 63
Tension, conveyance of voice, 102
Three Breaths, 34, 35, 37, 69, 215
Tickle monster effect, 135, 141
Timberlake, Justin, 220
Time
    playing with, 133–134
    taking, 168
Timing of intervention, 124
Tiredness, 46, 48
To-Do List, 38, 224
Tone
    high-pitched, melodic, 50
    lowering your, 102
    of your voice, 87, 88
Toning, vocal, 86–87, 91, 93, 94
Tough moments, getting through, 143
Transitional objects, 191
Transitions, 52
    use of music for, 198
Travarthen, Colwyn, 27, 117

V
Video camera, setting up in your home,
    27–28
Video microanalysis, 130–131
Visual cliff study, 98
Visual modality, 164, 165
Vocalizing, 86–91, 136
Vocal mirroring, 148, 150–155, 160
Vocal toning, 91, 93, 94
Voice, 83–95
    conveyance of tension in, 102
    faking your, 102
    high-pitched, melodic tone of, 50
    lower pitch of, 49
    not forgetting, 102

recognition of, 84–85
remembering, 102
to soothe baby, 88–91
sounds made by, 153–154
synthetic, 88
tone of your, 87, 88
use of, 13–14
wishes for, 90
Vowel O, 93

W
Waking up, 52
Welcoming words, 160–163

Wind-down, 189–190, 193
Winnicott, Donald, 191
    coining of "good-enough mother,"
        28
    coining of "potential space," 30
    creation of space and, 31
    Playing and Reality (book), 30
Witching hour, getting through, 215–
    229
Words, welcoming, 160–163

Y
"You Are My Sunshine" (song), 36